Introduction

At the start of World War II, the vulnerability of surface warships to attack from the air became obvious immediately. This resulted in all the warships that survived the initial onslaught being fitted with additional AA armament, as availability of both equipment and vessels, and space and weight margins, allowed. This usually took the form of adding the virtually useless quadruple 0.5in machine gun mounts and/or 2pdr (40mm) pom-pom mounts, carrying from one to eight barrels. These were gradually replaced with the more effective 20mm Oerlikon and 40mm Bofors guns as they became available.

This vulnerability was not a complete surprise to the Admiralty, the deficiencies in protection from air attack having emerged during the Abyssinian Crisis of 1935–36 when considering the threat of the Italian Air Force. The Admiralty had already initiated the development of more effective weapons, both the twin 4in and 5.25in mountings. They had also considered the construction of dedicated AA vessels but ran up against budget constraints, and so the conversion of existing vessels was considered. It was generally felt that vessels of destroyer size were too small and so investigations were carried out into cost-effective conversions of cruiser-size ships. Early proposals, in the mid-1930s, envisaged converting all the surviving 'C' class cruisers. It was intended that the 'D' and 'E' class vessels would be converted in a similar manner, at a later date, when suitable finance was available.

The first conversions were carried out in 1935–36, *Coventry* at Portsmouth Dockyard and *Curlew* at Chatham Dockyard, both members of the *Ceres* sub-class. They were to be fitted with ten single 4in guns, two eight-barrelled pom-pom mountings, and new fire control arrangements. In 1939, the second group of reconstructions (*Cairo* and *Calcutta* of the *Capetown* class) were very different as the twin 4in AA gun was now more readily available. *Carlisle* and *Curacoa* (*Capetown* and *Ceres* classes, respectively) followed, undergoing similar reconstructions. It was intended to convert *Capetown*, beginning in late 1939, but this was cancelled at the outbreak of war. The last two conversions (*Colombo* and *Caledon* of the *Capetown* and *Caledon* classes, respectively) were not started until after the war had begun and placed greater emphasis on self-protection, reducing the number of twin 4in mountings to three, releasing greater space for close-range weapons. Being the oldest vessel to receive this conversion, *Caledon* also required a number of modifications to the bridge structure to provide the required space. She ended her conversion looking virtually identical to *Colombo*, but could be distinguished as she had no sheer forward.

'C' CLASS

A total of twenty-eight 'C' class cruisers were launched between February 1914 and June 1919, being ordered and built in eight sub-classes. All were completed before the end of 1918, apart from the five vessels in the last sub-class, which were not completed until post-war. The primary armament of the first twelve vessels (three sub-classes) was two 6in guns, but this was increased to five for the later vessels. All those fitted with just two 6in guns, plus the first two fitted with five, were sold for breaking-up before the start of the Second World War, except for *Caroline*, the second to be launched, which still exists as a museum ship in Belfast.

With the exception of *Cassandra*, which was mined in December 1918, the remaining vessels all survived into the Second World War, where they all had active careers. The AA armament of these classes, as built, was very weak. The *Caledon* class (*Caledon*, *Calypso*, *Caradoc*) only carried two 3in Mk I AA guns and two 3pdr AA guns. The following *Ceres* (*Cardiff*, *Ceres*, *Coventry*, *Curacoa*, *Curlew*) and *Capetown* classes (*Cairo*, *Calcutta*, *Capetown*, *Carlisle*, *Colombo*) had two additional 2pdr pom-pom AA guns fitted on the centreline, at the aft

The museum ship HMS *Caroline* in Belfast, the last surviving 'C' class cruiser.

end of the superstructure between No 4 and No 5 turrets. Whilst all the other guns were on the centreline, the two 3pdr AA guns were sited abreast the fore-funnel, where they enjoyed wide firing arcs.

The *Ceres* class differed from the *Caledon* class in that the main armament was re-arranged, moving No 2 turret forward of the bridge, super-firing over No 1. This greatly increased the firing arc of No 2 turret and the forward fire of the cruiser. The bridge had to be moved aft and be raised, adversely affecting stability, and so the beam was increased by 8in. The *Capetown* class introduced the 'trawler' bow, increasing sheer forward to reduce wetness, a problem experienced by all 'C' class cruisers. The height at the stem was increased by 5ft. This was achieved by simply extending the side plating vertically from the existing deck edge, resulting in a distinctive knuckle. The overall length increased by fifteen inches.

Coventry. Built by Swan Hunter, Wallsend, Tyne and Wear, and launched in July 1917. In 1935, *Coventry* was nominated for reduction to reserve status and returned to Great Britain to pay-off. She was then selected for conversion to an anti-aircraft cruiser and taken in hand for conversion by HM Dockyard, Portsmouth in September. This refit involved the removal of her 6in guns and torpedo tubes, and the fitting of ten QF 4in Mk V guns on single Mk III high-angle mountings and two hydraulically-operated octuple-mounted 2pdr pom-pom guns, one in front of the bridge and one on the aft superstructure. The 4in weapons had previously been landed from other vessels.

The original fire control system and spotting top were to be removed and replaced by two HACS Mk III systems, one on the foremast and the other abaft the mainmast. Two platforms were fitted for pom-pom directors (although the directors themselves were not available at the time), on the centreline abaft the forward pom-

pom on an extension to the lower bridge platform, and abaft the aft HACS director. The fore topmast was to be removed, the director platform being replaced by a larger Air Direction Officer's platform, with the HA director. The mainmast was to be replaced by a lighter structure further forward, and the aft control position replaced by a 36in searchlight and a 12ft rangefinder, as compensation for the additional weight of the new equipment. Despite these measures, it was still necessary to add 100 tons of ballast.

A direction-finding office was fitted between the funnels, the aerials going between the office roof, the funnels and the ADO platform. Magazine arrangements were changed to accommodate the different calibre shells. Ready-use pom-pom lockers were provided on deck. Asdic Type 128 was added, with six depth charges in a single rack.

This refit lasted until October 1936 and on 15 November *Coventry* commissioned for trials. In January and February 1937, additional refit work was undertaken, including the actual fit of the multiple barrelled 2pdr pom-pom mountings, which had not been available earlier. From April onwards, she deployed for trials of new design equipment including degaussing gear and 20mm close-range Oerlikon guns.

The after pom-pom mounting was replaced by two quadruple Mk I mounts for the 0.5in Vickers Mk III machine gun before the start of WWII, and a director for the forward pom-pom was added. In July 1939 *Coventry*'s war station in the Mediterranean was allocated. In late 1939, the two 4in mounts abreast the fore-funnel were removed because of the adverse blast effect on other gun crews.

From February to April 1940, *Coventry* underwent a refit when the foremast was fitted with a topmast, and a metric air warning radar Type 279, with separate Tx and Rx antennas fitted on a tall mainmast, with an office fitted between the fore-funnel

▓ 'C' CLASS CRUISERS: PRINCIPAL PARTICULARS

	CALEDON CLASS	*CERES* CLASS	*CAPETOWN* CLASS
Names	*Caledon*	*Cardiff*	*Cairo*
	Calypso	*Ceres*	*Calcutta*
	Caradoc	*Coventry*	*Capetown*
	Cassandra	*Curacoa*	*Carlisle*
		Curlew	*Colombo*
Displacement (tons)			
Normal	4120	4190	4290
Deep Load	4950	5020	5250
Length Overall	450ft	450ft 3in	451ft 6in
Beam	42ft 9in	43ft 5in	43ft 6in
Machinery	2-shaft geared turbines, 40,000shp	2-shaft geared turbines, 40,000shp	2-shaft geared turbines, 40,000shp
Speed	29 knots	29 knots	29 knots
Primary Armament	Five 6in/45 cal Mk XII BL guns	Five 6in/45 cal Mk XII BL guns	Five 6in/45 cal Mk XII BL guns
Secondary Armament	Two 3in 20cwt Mk I AA guns	Two 3in 20cwt Mk I AA guns	Two 3in 20cwt Mk I AA guns
		Two 2pdr (40mm) 'pom-pom'	Two 2pdr (40mm) 'pom-pom'
Torpedo tubes	Four twin 21in mountings	Four twin 21in mountings	Four twin 21in mountings

and bridge. This required her forward AA director to be relocated to the fore end of her foretop. Splinter shields were fitted around her 4in guns. The two after 4in guns (Nos 6 and 7) were removed and a degaussing coil fitted.

On 16 June, she began a refit and docking on the Tyne at Wallsend, when her gun barrels were replaced. They were replaced again in April 1941, and from November to April 1942 *Coventry* underwent a refit, during which her boilers were re-tubed and she had a new bow fitted, after being torpedoed by the Italian submarine *Naiade*. She also carried five 20mm Oerlikon guns by May 1942 and two more were fitted at Alexandria in June.

In September 1942, *Coventry* was heavily damaged in the Eastern Mediterranean, northwest of Alexandria, by 16 German Junkers Ju 88 aircraft, whilst participating in Operation Agreement, a disastrous raid on Tobruk. The ship was set on fire and had to be scuttled by the destroyer *Zulu*.

Curlew was built by Vickers Limited, Barrow in Furness, being launched just one day before *Coventry*. In 1936 she was deployed in the Mediterranean, but in September she was nominated for return to Great Britain for conversion to an anti-aircraft cruiser. In October she made passage to Chatham to pay-off into dockyard control and in November she was taken in hand for conversion by the dockyard.

Her conversion was to be very similar to that of *Coventry*, but she was fitted with slightly less ballast, just 92 tons. As the forward pom-pom was sited further forward than that in *Coventry*, a separate pedestal was provided forward of the bridge for the forward pom-pom director. *Curlew* did not receive the 12ft rangefinder, just a 36in searchlight. *Curlew* also carried asdic Type 128 and depth charges. The same modifications were carried out before WWII, but *Curlew* also lost her searchlight platform and mainmast. In April 1937, she commissioned for trials.

In early 1939, *Curlew* was deployed as a training ship at Chatham. In July she was nominated for installation of a prototype aircraft warning radar outfit Type 79Z, which had been under development by HM Signal School Extension at Southsea since 1936. By August the installation of the radar was in hand at Chatham. This required changes to be made to both masts to accommodate the radar aerial units.

The war complement joined the ship and on 23 September the refit and installation works were completed. *Curlew* undertook radar trials on passage to Portland before sailing for to Scapa Flow to continue work-up and radar trials. On 21 October, she completed her work-up and deployed with the Home Fleet.

She participated in the Norwegian Campaign, and whilst operating off the Norwegian coast on 26 May 1940, she came under attack from German Junkers Ju 88 bombers and was sunk in Lavangsfjord, Ofotfjord near Narvik. Nine crew members were lost with the ship.

Cairo was built by Cammell Laird, being launched in November 1918. Whilst in reserve at Devonport, on 4 November 1937, *Cairo* was selected for conversion to an anti-aircraft cruiser. The conversion was intended to be carried out at Chatham, but this was subsequently changed and the work was done by HM Dockyard, Portsmouth.

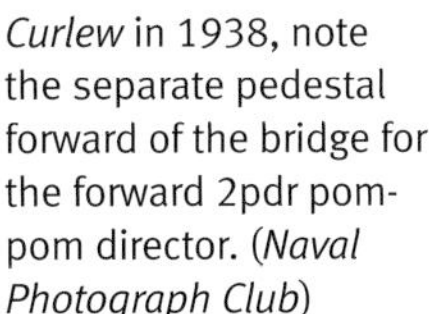

Curlew in 1938, note the separate pedestal forward of the bridge for the forward 2pdr pom-pom director. (*Naval Photograph Club*)

This view of *Cairo* after conversion clearly shows the forward twin 4in gun and 2pdr pom-pom mountings.

A close-up view of the port side of *Cairo*'s bridge, note the stowed Oropesa float.

The conversion was not as extensive as that carried out on *Coventry* and *Curlew*, but was arguably more effective. Four Mk XIX twin mountings for the 4in Mk XVI gun were fitted in the original 6in gun positions Nos 1, 3, 4 and 5. No 2' position was occupied by a quadruple pom-pom mounting Mk VIII. The 3in guns abreast the fore-funnel were removed and replaced by two quadruple Mk I mounts for the 0.5in Vickers Mk III machine gun.

The fire control equipment was removed and replaced by two HACS Mk III directors, one on the foremast and the other on the after superstructure. A pom-pom director was fitted on the compass platform. The aft control position was removed and two 36in searchlights were fitted 'en echelon' on either side of the superstructure, just forward of the aft HACS director. The pole mainmast was replaced by a tripod mast, with a direction-finding antenna at the top. The torpedo tubes were removed and the

magazines modified; 111 tons of ballast were fitted.

On 26 April 1940, *Cairo* was taken in hand for refit by HM Dockyard, Rosyth, and on 1 June she had repairs undertaken by Palmers at Hebburn. In July a Type 279 metric radar for aircraft warning was fitted, and in January/February 1941, whilst under repair and refit on the Tyne, Type 285 ranging radar for the main AA armament was fitted. In April *Cairo* had her boiler tubes replaced whilst on the Clyde. In March 1942, a Type 271 centimetric radar for surface warning was fitted at Belfast.

On 15 June, she was seriously damaged by two 6in shells from Italian cruisers and was repaired at Gibraltar. In August 1942, *Cairo* took part in Operation Pedestal, a convoy to Malta. On the 12th, she was torpedoed by the Italian submarine *Axum* north of Bizerta, Tunisia. One torpedo blew off part of the stern, the port propeller was detached, the engine room flooded and gun mount No 5 fell into the sea. During the battle it was impossible to tow her to safety, and so it was decided to scuttle her. The destroyer *Pathfinder* fired four torpedoes but only one hit. A series of depth charges did not sink her, so the escort destroyer *Derwent* received orders to sink her with gunfire. Twenty-four members of the crew were lost.

Calcutta. Built by Vickers Limited, Barrow-in-Furness and launched on 9 July 1918. In August 1938 she started her conversion at Chatham Dockyard. The conversion was virtually identical to that of *Cairo* and was completed in July 1939. Following conversion, *Calcutta* carried out post conversion trials in the Nore Command area and then joined the Home Fleet in August 1939. In July 1940 she was under repair on the Tyne. The after HACS was scheduled for fitting but was not available so it was planned to be added in 1942.

During the evacuation of Allied forces from Crete in 1941, *Calcutta* and *Coventry* set out from Alexandria on 1 June to provide extra anti-aircraft protection for the cruiser *Phoebe* and other ships returning

Calcutta wearing a complicated camouflage pattern, shortly before being sunk.

with troops from Sphakia, but about 100 nautical miles north-west of Alexandria the two ships were attacked by two Junkers Ju 88 bombers, which dived out of the sun, giving little warning. *Calcutta* was hit by two bombs and sank, with 255 men being rescued by *Coventry* and 107 men killed or missing.

Carlisle was built by the Fairfield Shipbuilding and Engineering Company, Glasgow, being launched on 9 July 1918. In March 1937 she returned to Great Britain to be reduced to reserve, and in January 1939, she started her conversion to an anti-aircraft cruiser at HM Dockyard Devonport, with eight 4in QF Mk XVI guns on twin mounts, and one quadruple 2pdr pom-pom being fitted. This conversion was completed in January 1940, and *Carlisle* was fitted with Army Type GL Mark 2 radar for detection of aircraft at long ranges. This equipment was designated radar Type 280 combined air warning and gunnery radar when used by the RN; she thus became the first naval vessel to be equipped with an anti-aircraft fire control radar system.

Carlisle then carried out radar trials in the Mediterranean based in Malta and in March took passage to return to Scapa Flow. She then joined the 1st AA Squadron, deployed in Humber Force, Home Fleet. In September 1940 *Carlisle* underwent a refit at Colombo.

In March 1941, she was taken in hand for repair at Alexandria. A defective shaft was taken to Malta by submarine for repair in HM Dockyard. On 25 May *Carlisle* resumed repair at Port Said, after the repaired shaft had been returned by submarine from Malta. No 2 AA mounting was replaced. In July 1942 she was taken in hand for a refit by HM Dockyard,

Devonport. The work, carried out between August and November, included the replacement of the aircraft warning radar Type 280 by Type 281, surmounted by Type 241 IFF, and installation of centimetric surface warning radar Type 273. AA fire control radars Type 285 for the 4in mountings and Type 282 for the pom-pom were also fitted. *Carlisle* also carried five twin 20mm Oerlikon mountings in addition to the quad pom-pom mounting. She was nominated for service in the Mediterranean, where she returned after post-refit trials.

On 9 October 1943, *Carlisle* came under air attack by Ju 87s during a patrol in the Scarpanto Strait with the destroyers *Panther* and *Rockwood*. She received four direct hits and several near misses which caused extensive structural damage and flooding. The starboard shaft and propeller were blown off and the port shaft was buckled. Disabled with twenty of the ship's company killed and seventeen wounded, the stricken vessel was taken in tow to Alexandria by *Rockwood*. In November, *Carlisle* was declared a constructive total loss and converted for use as a base ship for escort vessels at Alexandria. She was not paid off until after VJ Day and in 1949 was placed on the Disposal List. The ship was then sold and broken up locally at Alexandria.

Curacoa was built at Pembroke Dockyard in Wales, being launched on 5 May 1917. In July 1939 she began her conversion at Chatham Dockyard, having served as a training ship since 1933. The changes to her gun armament were the same as for *Cairo*, and her torpedo tubes were removed. Likewise her masts were cut down and her existing fire-control systems were replaced by a pair of HACS Mk III systems and a

This photo of *Carlisle* in 1942 clearly shows both her camouflage pattern and the disposition of her main armament mountings, together with numerous aerials.

Curacoa in 1942. With the barrels of the main armament at the same elevation (including the 2pdr pom-pom forward), it is easy to see the positions of the mountings.

pom-pom. A Type 279 early-warning radar, with separate transmit and receive antennas, was also installed. To counter the additional weight high in the ship, 200 tons of ballast were added. Although the weight of the ballast alone was more than that of the new equipment, *Curacoa*'s metacentric height still increased from 2.93 to 3.41 feet at deep load. Her conversion was completed on 24 January 1940 and *Curacoa* was assigned to the Home Fleet.

On 22 April she deployed at Andalsnes, Norway for AA guardship duties and on the 24th, after repelling heavy and sustained air attacks on the area following her arrival, *Curacoa* was hit by a bomb below the bridge structure and sustained major damage. Withdrawn from guardship duty, she took passage to Great Britian for repair under her own steam, escorted by the sloop *Flamingo*. Thirty of the ship's company were killed and another thirty wounded.

On 2 May she arrived at HM Dockyard, Chatham, but the repair was delayed by the accumulation of higher priority work, and did not begin until July. Post-refit trials took place in August. From April to June 1941, she was under repair in HM Dockyard, Rosyth. Twelve months later,

Curacoa was again under refit at Rosyth, which included the installation of the surface warning radar Type 271 and the fire control radar Type 282 for the close-range AA armament.

On the morning of 2 October 1942, *Curacoa* rendezvoused north of Ireland with the ocean liner RMS *Queen Mary*, which was carrying approximately 10,000 American troops. To counter submarine attacks, the liner was steaming an evasive 'zig-zag Pattern No 8' course at a speed of 28½ knots, which resulted in an overall rate of advance of 26½ knots. *Curacoa* remained on a straight course at a top speed of 25 knots and would eventually be overtaken by the liner.

Both captains believed they had right of way under the international Rule of the Road. *Curacoa* kept to the liner's mean course to maximise her ability to defend the liner from enemy aircraft, while *Queen Mary* continued her zig-zag pattern. At 1332, during the zig-zag, it became apparent that *Queen Mary* would come very close to the cruiser and the liner's officer of the watch interrupted her zig-zag to avoid *Curacoa*. However, her captain, Commodore Illingworth, told his officer to 'Carry on with the zig-zag. These chaps are used to escorting; they will keep out of your way and won't interfere with you.' At 1404, *Queen Mary* started a starboard turn from a position slightly behind the cruiser and at a distance of two cables. *Curacoa*'s captain, Boutwood, perceived the danger, but the distance was too close for either of the hard turns ordered for each ship to make any difference at the speeds that they were travelling. *Queen Mary* struck *Curacoa* amidships at full speed, cutting the cruiser in half. The aft end sank almost immediately, but the rest of the ship stayed on the surface a few minutes longer. By way of explanation, it is thought that the liner was under threat of attack by *U407*, which was sighted visually and, in an attempt to prevent an approach by the submarine, *Curacoa* crossed the zig-zag path of *Queen Mary*.

Acting under orders not to stop due to the risk of U-boat attacks, *Queen Mary* steamed onwards with a damaged bow. She radioed the destroyers of her escort, about 7nm away, and reported the collision. Some hours later, the convoy's escorts, *Bramham* and *Cowdray*, returned to rescue approximately 101 survivors, including Boutwood. Lost with *Curacoa* were 337 officers and men of her crew. Those who witnessed the collision were sworn to secrecy due to national security concerns and the loss was not publicly reported until after the war ended. The Admiralty did file a writ against the *Queen Mary*'s owners, Cunard White Star Line, on 22 September 1943 in the Admiralty Court of the High Court of Justice. The case did not go to trial until June 1945 and it was adjourned to November and then to December 1946. The court exonerated *Queen Mary*'s crew and her owners from blame on 21 January 1947 and laid all fault on *Curacoa*'s officers. The Admiralty appealed this ruling and the Court of Appeal modified the judgment, assigning two-thirds of the blame to the Admiralty and one-third to Cunard White Star. The latter appealed to the House of Lords, but the decision was upheld.

Colombo was built by Fairfield Shipbuilding and Engineering Company, being launched on 18 December 1918. She spent the early part of WWII in service with the Home Fleet, during which time she captured the German merchant ship *Henning Oldendorff*.

In January 1942, while serving in the Indian Ocean, she was selected for conversion for use as an anti-aircraft cruiser and in May took passage to Great Britain, arriving at Plymouth on 5 June and paid off into Dockyard Control for the necessary work. The conversion took from July until December. The original armament was replaced by three twin 4in AA mountings, two forward and one aft, with HACS Mk III with radar Type 285 for fire-control, two twin 40mm Bofors 'Hazemeyer' mountings

Colombo in June 1943. Note the twin 20mm guns fitted forward of the aft twin 4in mounting.

were fitted abaft the aft funnel and six twin 20mm Oerlikon guns in Mk V mountings were added for close range defence against aircraft. These were sited in pairs, either side of the fore-funnel, either side of the searchlight platform and on either side on the aft superstructure. Two single 20mm guns were fitted in the bridge wings. Type 279 aircraft warning radar was fitted on the mainmast and Type 273 surface warning radar abaft the mainmast on the centre line. Both pole masts were replaced with tripods.

In February 1943, *Colombo* carried out post-refit trials and recommissioned for service in the Mediterranean. In March 1945 she was nominated for reduction to reserve and to be withdrawn from operational service in the Mediterranean, taking passage to Great Britain in April. In July, *Colombo* was laid-up in reserve at Dartmouth, where she remained until placed on the Disposal List in 1947. The vessel was sold to BISCO for breaking-up by J J Cashmore on 22 January 1948, and arrived in tow at the breaker's yard in Newport on 15 May 1948.

Caledon was built by Cammell Laird, being launched on 25 November 1916. In the Second World War, following involvement in the campaign against Japan, she underwent conversion at Chatham Dockyard between 14 September 1942 and 7 December 1943, when her former armament was replaced by three QF 4in Mk XVI twin and two Bofors 40mm Mk IV 'Hazemeyer' twin mounts. Aircraft warning radar Type 279, surface warning radar Type 272 and fire-control radars Type 285 and Type 282 were fitted. By 1944 the armament had been supplemented by six Bofors 40mm Mk III and one Oerlikon 20mm Mk III single mounts.

As *Caledon* was a member of the earliest 'C' class to be converted, the locations of her original armament were different to those of *Colombo*, and so considerable rearrangement of the forward superstructure/bridge area was required; 200 tons of

This view of *Caledon* in December 1943 clearly shows the two twin 4in, mountings forward, the director control tower and the cut-down foremast; note the perspex protective cylinder on the radar aft of the mainmast.

ballast were added, giving a total displacement of 5320 tons full load.

In January 1945, whilst deployed in Greek waters, she was nominated for withdrawal from operational service. She paid off in March, being laid up at Falmouth. *Caledon* was used for target trials and then placed on the Disposal List. She was sold to BISCO on 22 January 1948 and arrived at Dover for breaking up on 14 February.

'D' CLASS CRUISER *DELHI*

The Admiralty's plans pre-war included modifying the 'D' and 'E' class cruisers in a similar manner to those of the 'C' class, but financial limitations, and the advent of the war itself, stopped these plans coming to fruition. However, the 'D' class cruiser *Delhi* did receive a very different modification in 1941, being fitted with American armament and fire control, thus allowing a direct comparison to be made between technological developments in the USA and Great Britain.

Delhi was built by Armstrong Whitworth, being launched on 23 August 1918. The 'D' class were larger than the proceeding 'C' class, with an overall length of 471ft, a beam of 45½ft and a draught of 16½ft. Displacement was 4970 tons standard, 5870 tons deep. She was driven by Brown-Curtis geared turbines, producing 40,000shp, for a maximum speed of 29 knots. Like the *Capetown* class, *Delhi* received a 'trawler' bow to reduce wetness.

The increase in size permitted the fitting of another 6in gun, and triple torpedo tubes in place of twins. The armament, as-built, was therefore six 6in breech loading guns Mk XII ('A', 'B', 'P', 'Q', 'X', 'Y' mounts) on CPXIV mounts, two 3in Mk I AA guns abreast the fore-funnel, two 2pdr 'pom-poms' on the aft superstructure, abaft No 5 gun and twelve torpedo tubes. Between the wars, the entire class had their anti-aircraft armament standardised as three QF 4in Mk V guns on HA Mk III mountings (two replaced the 3in guns and the third was fitted abaft No 5 gun), with a QF 2pdr Mk II gun in each bridge wing. Early modifications in WWII included the addition of air warning radar Type 286 at the foremast head and, later, Type 273 centimetric target indication set on the searchlight platform amidships. Between six and eight 20mm Oerlikon guns were added, replacing the old 2pdr guns in the bridge wings, on either side of 'P' and 'Q' guns and on the quarterdeck.

Extensive discussions between the Americans and the British led to *Delhi* being rebuilt at the Norfolk Navy Yard as an anti-aircraft vessel, between May and December 1941. As well as the new equipment, she received a complete refit of her hull and machinery. As the American equipment used AC power, many changes were

Delhi in December 1941 having just been fitted with the American 5in guns and fire control systems, before receiving camouflage.

required to the electrical system to replace the British DC system.

All armaments were removed, and five 5in/38-cal Mk 12 guns in Mk 30 single mountings were added, controlled by a pair of Mk 37 Fire Control Systems. The guns were originally intended for the USS *Edison* (DD-439), and were mounted in all but the former 'P' position, the directors being fitted on the compass platform and abaft the mainmast. A new bridge structure was added and she stepped light tripod masts fore and aft, carrying Type 291 air warning radar. A Type 273 target indication radar was added amidships and a Type 285 on the Mk 37 FCS for target ranging and bearings. The light armament consisted of two quadruple 2pdr mounts Mk VII and their directors with radar Type 282 on each side of the fore-funnel, and eight single Mk III Oerlikon pedestal mounts, two in the bridge wings, two between the funnels, two abaft the mainmast and two on the after superstructure.

The British radar equipment was fitted after *Delhi* returned to Great Britain. An office for the FM2 direction finding equipment was fitted between the funnels, with the aerial on the roof, and two 36in searchlights were fitted forward of the fore-funnel.

At this time, *Delhi* carried 200 tons of ballast to maintain stability.

Delhi subsequently supported landings both in Italy and the south of France, but on 12 February 1945, she was attacked by German explosive motorboats in the harbour at Split, Croatia. The attack missed *Delhi* but the force of the resulting explosion damaged her rudder and a propeller shaft bracket. She returned to Great Britain and was laid up after the war. Because of her age, she was assessed as uneconomic to repair, and was instead sold on 22 January 1948 to be broken-up, arriving at the yards of Cashmore, of Newport, Wales, in April 1948 to be scrapped.

AUXILIARY ANTI-AIRCRAFT SHIPS

In order to provide additional means of anti-aircraft defence, the Royal Navy also requisitioned and fitted out a number of mercantile vessels to act as Auxiliary Anti-Aircraft Ships. The Admiralty had already taken some steps in this direction by specifying some basic requirements – to be armed with the Mk XVI 4in gun on the Mk XIX twin mounting; self-defence to be provided by quadruple 0.5in machine guns and 2pdr

Jeanie Deans as originally converted to a minesweeper.

Goatfell after conversion to an auxiliary AA ship in 1941.

(40mm) pom-poms; to be fitted with diesel engines to provide suitable speed and sufficient range for the task envisaged, *ie* convoy escort.

The first to be taken up was ***Jeanie Deans*** (J108 as minesweeper, then 4.29), which was commissioned on 29 October 1939. She was a Clyde paddle steamer, built for the London and North Eastern Railway by Fairfield Shipbuilding & Engineering Co, Govan and launched on 7 April 1931, being completed later that year. Her length was 250ft 6in, her beam 30ft 1in, and she displaced 635 tons GRT. The *Jeanie Deans* had a maximum speed of just 14 knots, although she had achieved a speed of 18.5 knots on trials.

Requisitioned by the Admiralty in September 1939, she was initially converted to a minesweeper but in April 1941, she went to the Royal Albert Dock in London for conversion to an anti-aircraft vessel, entering service in the following month in the Thames Local Defence Flotilla. She was based at Sheerness, operating from the Humber to the Thames Estuary. She was fitted with four single 2pdr guns, four single 20mm guns, eight 0.5in MG in two quadruple mountings, and sixteen 0.303in MG in four quadruple mountings. *Jeanie Deans* was paid off on 17 April 1945, being returned to her owner in May 1946.

Early in the war she was joined by ***Goatfell*** (J125, then 4.36), which was commissioned on 13 December. Originally named PS *Caledonia, Goatfell* had been

Emperor of India as an AA ship.

built by William Denny & Brothers, Dumbarton, and was launched on 1 February 1934. She was slightly smaller at 230ft long, with a beam of 62ft and a displacement of 428 tons GRT, and had principally provided an Upper Clyde ferry service before being requisitioned in September 1939. *Goatfell* had a maximum speed of 16.5 knots.

Like *Jeanie Deans*, she was initially converted to a minesweeper but in 1941 was converted to an anti-aircraft vessel. Her armament was similar and comprised four single 2pdr guns, six single 20mm guns, eight 0.5in MG in two quadruple mountings. This slightly lighter armament was supplemented by four single 3in rocket launchers. She became an accommodation ship in 1944, and in 1946 *Caledonia* was returned to her owners.

Originally named *Southend Belle*, **Laguna Belle** (J112, R373, then 4.373), also requisitioned in September 1939, was a much older passenger ship, having been built by William Denny & Brothers, Dumbarton, for the London, Woolwich and Clacton-on-Sea Steamboat Co, being launched on 6 March 1896. Her top speed was higher than the previous vessels, at 18 knots, and she was 249ft long with a beam of 30ft and a displacement of 570 tons GRT.

She was initially converted to an Auxiliary Paddle Minesweeper and armed with one 12pdr gun and light AA guns. In 1942 she was converted to an anti-aircraft vessel, retaining her 12pdr gun and being fitted with two single 2pdr guns, four single 20mm guns, and four single 3in rocket launchers. *Laguna Belle* became an accommodation ship in January 1944, and was scrapped in the Netherlands in late 1946.

The paddle steamer *Princess Royal* was built for the Southampton, Isle of Wight & South of England Royal Mail Steam Packet Co, by J I Thornycroft, Woolston, in 1906. Later she was lengthened by 21ft 8in to 217ft 2in to increase her speed, sold to Cosens & Co of Weymouth and renamed **Emperor of India**. She had a beam of 25ft 1in, a displacement of 428 tons GRT, and a top speed in excess of 15 knots.

During World War I she served as a trooper and minesweeper in the Mediterranean as HMS *Mahratta*. She was requisitioned in September 1939 and commissioned on 12 March 1940 as *Emperor of India* (J106, R237 then 4.237). Her armament comprised two single 2pdr guns, two quadruple 0.5in MG mountings and four single 3in rocket launchers. She was placed on Harbour Service as of 1943 and renamed *Bunting* in 1944. She was returned to her owner and renamed *Emperor of India* in 1945.

HMS Foylebank was a 5582-ton merchant ship that was built for the Bank Line (Andrew Weir Shipping), by Harland & Wolff Ltd, Belfast, and launched on 12 June 1930. She had a top speed of 11 knots.

Requisitioned in September 1939, she was converted into an anti-aircraft ship, equipped with 0.5in machine guns, two quad 2pdr pom-poms and four twin high angle 4in gun mountings, and commissioned on 6 June 1940. Her active career was short; she was attacked by 26 Junkers Ju 87 Stukas at Portland on 4 July 1940. *Foylebank* destroyed two of the dive-bombers, but 176 personnel were killed and all but 40 of her crew of approximately 300 were wounded. The survivors included her commanding officer, Capt (ret) Henry Percival Wilson, RN. One of the ship's company, Jack Foreman Mantle, was posthumously awarded the Victoria Cross for his actions in defending the ship from aircraft whilst mortally injured. *Foylebank* sank the next day.

The motor vessel **Alynbank** was also built for the Bank Line (Andrew Weir & Co, Glasgow) by Harland & Wolff Ltd, Govan, in 1925. She had a length of 420ft, a beam of

Foylebank. The substantial nature of the conversion can be seen in the additional decks fore and aft for the twin 4in mountings, along with a naval-style bridge.

Alynbank was given a very similar conversion to her Bank Line sister *Foylebank*, producing a ship with similar AA capabilities to the 'C' class cruiser conversions, although lacking the speed and protection of a genuine warship.

This aerial view of *Alynbank* in 1941 gives a clear idea of the radically altered topside layout of the auxiliary AA ships, with additional superstructure fore and aft to give the 4in twin mountings good sky arcs, and a naval-style block bridge topped by a HA director.

53ft, a draught of 11ft and a displacement of 5151 tons GRT.

She was requisitioned in April 1940 and commissioned on 16 June 1940 as HMS *Alynbank* (F84). Her armament comprised four twin 4in gun mountings and two quadruple 2pdr gun mountings. She escorted numerous PQ and QP convoys, including the infamous PQ17, and supported operations in North Africa. *Alynbank* was sunk as part of Gooseberry No 3 Harbour at Arromanches on 9 June 1944.

The conversion of **HMCS *Prince Robert*** to an Armed Merchant Cruiser (AMC) by the Royal Canadian Navy was completed on 3 August 1940, the term AMC usually being applied to merchantmen carrying only surface weapons. She was paid off to be refitted as an anti-aircraft cruiser on 2 January 1943 and recommissioned as such in Montreal on 7 June 1943, and assigned the pendant number F56. She had been built by Cammell Laird Shipyard, Birkenhead, and was the first of three refrigerated passenger and cargo ships constructed for the Canadian National Railway. Completed in August 1930, she was 385ft overall, had a beam of 57ft and a displacement of 6893 tons GRT. Her top speed was in excess of 22 knots.

Her earlier conversion to an AMC included the trunking of the three funnels into two shorter ones, the installation of four breech-loading 6in Mk VII guns, one on each of the two decks forward and aft. The 6in guns had been provided by the Royal Navy and had once been part of the armament of *King Edward VII* class battleships. Two 3in guns were fitted on the upper deck amidships along with light anti-aircraft machine guns. Two depth charge chutes were placed over the stern, though no antisubmarine warfare detection equipment was provided. As an anti-aircraft ship, her main armament consisted of ten 4in QF Mk XVI high-angle/low-angle dual-purpose

guns in five twin mountings. Furthermore, the ship was given eight 2pdr pom-poms in two quadruple mounts and twelve 20mm Oerlikon guns. *Prince Robert* was also fitted with four depth charge throwers.

Prince Robert decommissioned on 10 December 1945, and was sold into mercantile service in 1948, being renamed *Charlton Sovereign*. Resold in 1953, she became the Italian *Lucania* and was scrapped in 1952.

Pozarica was completed in January 1938 by Doxford Shipyard, Sunderland. She had a displacement of 1893 tons GRT. She was requisitioned in August 1940 and, when commissioned on 3 July 1941 as HMS *Pozarica* (4.261), she carried an armament of three twin 4in turrets and two quadruple 2pdr pom-pom mountings.

During the afternoon of 29 January 1943, *Pozarica* was escorting the coastal convoy TF.14, running between Algerian ports. Off Bougie, the convoy was attacked by two squadrons of torpedo planes, one made up of thirteen German aircraft (ten He 111 and three Ju 88), and the other consisting of eight Italian S.79 aircraft. The destroyer *Avon Vale* was hit by the German aircraft and *Pozarica* was hit by the Italian planes. *Avon Vale* ran herself aground with the bows totally wrecked, while *Pozarica*, was hit near the stern and managed to reach Bougie roads.

On 13 February, while under salvage, *Pozarica* suddenly capsized and settled on the bottom. The wreck was refloated postwar and towed to Italy for scrapping, beginning in May 1951.

Springbank (F50) was originally a cargo ship (length of 420ft 4in, a beam of 53ft 11in, and a displacement of 5155 tons GRT) that was built in 1926 by Harland & Wolff Ltd, Govan, for the Bank Line. She was acquired by the Admiralty at the start of the war and converted to an auxiliary anti-aircraft cruiser by the addition of four twin 4in mountings and two quadruple 2pdr pom-poms.

In March 1941 a catapult, for a single Fairey Fulmar naval fighter, was fitted midships as a means of giving some protection for convoys from enemy aircraft. In this form, *Springbank* formed part of the escort for Convoy HG73 from Gibraltar to Liverpool. Her Fulmar was launched to drive off a German Focke-Wulf FW200 reconnaissance aircraft, the Fulmar landing at Gibraltar afterwards. The convoy was attacked by Italian and German submarines over the following days, and during the night of 27 September 1941 *Springbank* was torpedoed by the German submarine *U-201*. After taking off her surviving crew, the ship was sunk by the 'Flower' class corvette *Jasmine*.

Originally MV **Palomares**, built by William Doxford & Sons, Sunderland in 1937, operated as a merchant fruit carrier

Prince Robert, with five twin 4in mountings, was the most powerful of the AA conversions.

Pozarica was one of a pair of small fast fruit carriers given substantial conversions for their new AA role.

ship for service with the MacAndrews Line on their Spanish service. She was purchased by the Admiralty in 1940, as these fruit ships were considered to be fast and manoeuvrable. *Palomares* had a displacement of 1896 tons GRT and a maximum speed of 13.5 knots.

In 1941 the Admiralty converted her to an anti-aircraft ship (F98) and in December 1942 to a fighter direction ship. Upon conversion to an anti-aircraft ship, *Palomares* was equipped with six 4in AA guns in three twin mountings and eight 2pdr (40mm) pom-poms in two quadruple mounts.

In November 1941, *Palomares* was involved in the operation that resulted in the sinking of the aircraft carrier *Ark Royal*. She also took part in convoys to and from Russia, including the infamous PQ17, and in October 1942 *Palomares* participated in convoys in support of the landings at Algiers and Oran during Operation Torch.

Surviving the war, *Palomares* was returned to the MacAndrews Line in 1946, where she continued service with the company until 1959. She was then sold, and in October 1961, following a fire, she drifted aground and was wrecked.

Another ship involved in supporting the landings at Algiers and Oran was **Tynwald**. The following month, she also supported Operation Perpetual, the landings at Bougie.

Tynwald had been built by Vickers Armstrong, Barrow-in-Furness, being launched in December 1936 and completed in June 1937. She was a passenger vessel which served with the Isle of Man Steam Packet Company from 1937 until she was requisitioned for war service at the end of 1940. *Tynwald* had a gross registered tonnage of 2376, a beam of 46ft, a length of 314ft 6in, a draught of 18ft and a design speed of 21 knots. She had crew accommodation for 68, and a capacity for 1968 passengers. Commissioned on 1 October 1941, HMS *Tynwald* (D69) was armed with six 4in AA guns in three twin mountings and eight 2pdr (40mm) AA guns in two quad mounts.

After a year on convoy escort duties around Britain, including the evacuation of troops from Dunkirk, where she earned the distinction of embarking more troops than any other company vessel, she was assigned to Operation Torch, the Allied landing in North Africa.

During that operation, in the early morning of 12 November 1942, *Tynwald*

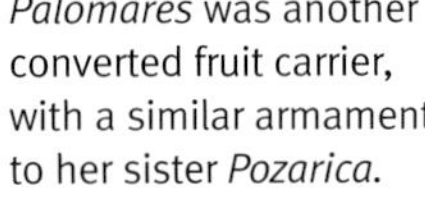

was at short notice, ready to sail from 0445 hrs onwards, in the expectation of an Axis air raid at dawn. She was anchored next to the monitor *Roberts*. Approximately 30 minutes later, she was hit by two torpedoes fired by the Italian submarine *Argo*. *Tynwald* settled rapidly in 7 metres of water with 10 dead, survivors being rescued by *Roberts* and the corvette *Samphire*.

The Belfast Steamship Co received three 3700-ton diesel powered ships, built by Harland and Wolff, between 1929 and 1930. These were the world's first diesel cross-channel ships and **Ulster Queen** was the second of these, being launched on 28 March 1929 and completed on 11 February 1930. She had a length of 345ft, a beam of 46ft and a draught of 13½ft, with a GRT of 3756 tons. The installed power from two 10-cylinder airless injection engines gave her a top speed of 17 knots.

She was requisitioned by the Admiralty in August 1940 and substantially modified. Her boat deck and one funnel were removed

Tynwald, a converted short-sea passenger vessel, had a maximum speed of 21 knots, which made her significantly faster than the cargo ship conversions.

Ulster Queen on 8 June 1943. She was one of the most heavily modified of the AA conversions, presenting a warship-like profile when commissioned.

and armour plating was added to the hull. When she commissioned on 26 July 1941 (pendant number F118), she had an armament of six 4in, in three twin mountings, eight 2pdr pom-poms (40mm) in two quadruple mountings, and ten single 20mm AA guns. She was purchased outright by the Admiralty and served with the Russian convoys, in the Mediterranean and in the Far East. Later, *Ulster Queen* became a fighter direction ship in 1943, before being paid off on 1 April 1946. The modifications were too substantial for her to return to passenger service and so she was laid-up, and eventually scrapped in 1950.

■ ANTI-AIRCRAFT GUNS: PRINCIPAL PARTICULARS

Coventry, one of the pair (with *Curlew*) of prototype anti-aircraft cruiser conversions, as recommissioned in 1936. The principal AA weapon was the 4in Mk V gun on Mk III single mountings, very evident in this port quarter view of the ship. Ten were carried: one forward, six sided amidships, and three aft. Close-range defence was provided by two multiple 2pdr pom-pom mountings, one 8-barrelled forward and one quad on the after superstructure. Later conversions utilised the twin Mk XIX mounting, which was heavier and required more deck space, so only eight (and later six) 4in Mk XVI guns were carried. (*James Fahey collection, US Naval Institute*)

	Mk V gun in Mk III mounting	Mk XVI gun in Mk XIX mounting	Mk I gun in Mk III UD mounting	Mk 12 gun in Mk 30 mounting	Mk II gun in Mk II mounting
Country of manufacture	GB	GB	GB	USA	GB
GUN DATA					
Bore	4in	4in	4.45in	5in	5.25in
Length (o.a.)	187.8in	190.5in	211.75in	223.75in	275.5in
Twist	1 in 30	1 in 30	1 in 25	1 in 30	1 in 30
Projectile weight	31lb	35lb	55lb	55lb	80lb
Muzzle velocity	2387ft/sec	2660ft/sec	2449ft/sec	2600ft/sec	2672ft/sec
Approximate life	850 EFC	600 EFC	750 EFC	4600 EFC	750 EFC
Maximum range	26,430yds at 44°	19,850yds at 45°	20,750yds at 45°	18,200yds at 45°	24,070yds at 45°
Ceiling	31,000ft at 80°	39,000ft at 80°	41,000ft at 80°	37,200ft at 85°	46,500ft at 70°
MOUNTING DATA					
Number of barrels	1	2	2	1	2
Weight	7 tons	16 tons	29.7 tons	18.37 tons	90 tons
Elevation range	-5° to +80°	-10° to +80°	-5° to +80°	-15° to +85°	-5° to +70°
Elevating speed	Hand worked	Hand worked 3° per revolution	Hand worked	18°/sec	10°/sec
Training range	360°	340° or 670°	+150°/-150	328°	+150°/-150
Training speed	Hand worked	Hand worked 4° per revolution	Hand worked	34°/sec	10°/sec
Firing cycle		5 sec		4 sec	5-6 sec

Model Products

NAVIS-NEPTUN
1:1250 scale

This well-known German company produces a very wide range of metal models at 1:1250 scale, the range being so large that not all models can be in production simultaneously, frequently leading to delays when ordering models of specific vessels. They are normally painted grey overall, with limited highlights such as

black tops to funnels and brown decks for boats. A limited number of models are available in camouflage colours.

Of specific relevance are 1149a *Cairo* (1940), 1149b *Curlew* (1940), 1148 *Delhi* (1943), 1141 *Dido* (1940), 1141a *Scylla* (1941) and 1141b *Black Prince* (1943).

Far left: *Curlew*
Left: *Black Prince*

COMBRIG
1:700 scale

The Russian company Combrig produces three waterline resin kits of *Caledon*, at different times in her career. These are 1917, 1923 & 1941, *ie* before her conversion to an anti-aircraft cruiser in 1943. For modellers wishing to represent *Caledon* at this later time, a significant amount of 'scratch-building' will be necessary. The twin 4in guns are available from a number of sources, such as Micro Models of New Zealand.

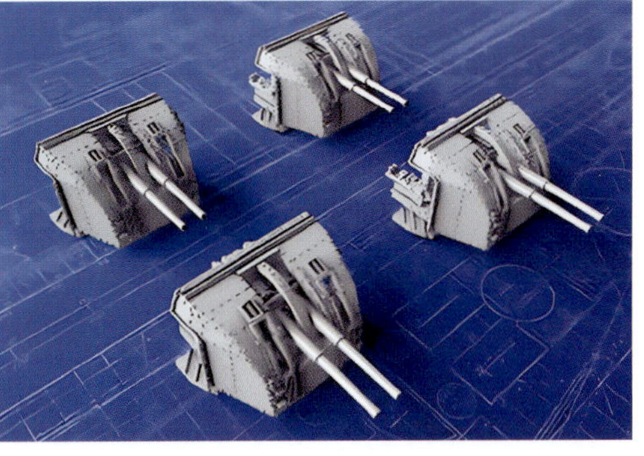

Micro Models twin 4in mountings

also an etched brass sheet, the same one for all three models, with guardwires, funnel grilles, ladders and other details. Instructions comprise a general arrangement, illustrations of the components and three assembly diagrams, but no colour details.

These Combrig kits are similar – a waterline hull with integral major superstructure parts, 16 sprues, containing gun mountings, funnels, boats, etc, and a resin wafer, containing superstructure decks. There is

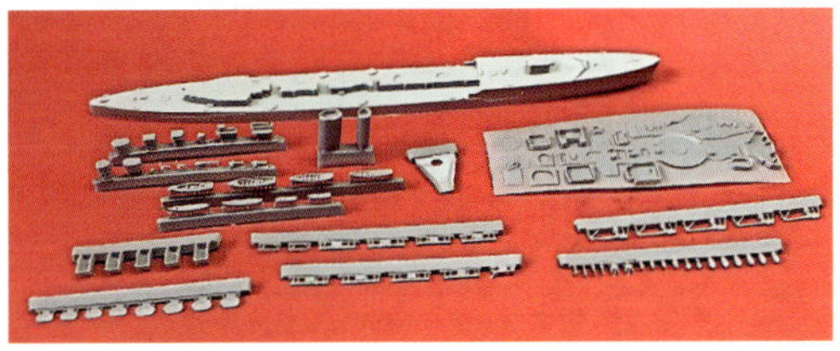

HP MODELS
1:700 scale

The HP Models kits are no longer available, but they were resin waterline kits, with only a limited number of parts for the superstructure, boats and armament. There was no etched brass but diagrams for

the masts identified both lengths and diameters of the parts, brass rod to be provided by the modeller. The instructions consisted of an arrangement drawing, an overall assembly diagram and colour details.

The four kits were of *Coventry* in 1940, *Curlew* in 1938, *Calcutta* in 1939 and *Colombo* in 1943. Only *Colombo* is illustrated in camouflage, the colours being identified by their Admiralty numbers – 507A, MS2, B5 and MS4a.

AJM MODELS

1:700 scale

This Polish company produces two models of this class of cruiser – *Cardiff* (1943) and *Coventry* (1942). *Cardiff* never received a conversion and so still retains her 6in guns although her AA armament has been enhanced. *Coventry* is depicted as an AA cruiser.

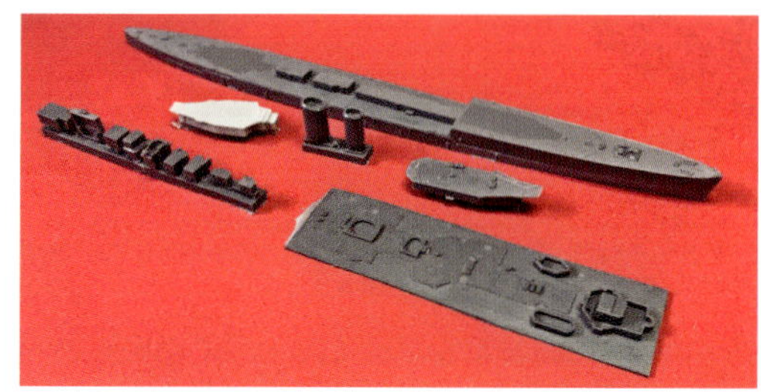

Coventry contains a resin waterline hull, a resin wafer with the other decks, and two plastic bags containing the smaller parts, including two superstructure blocks and the two funnels. Each resin casting is simple, resulting in numerous small parts and a lot of assembly work. For example, the 4in gun is assembled from 13 individual parts and the 'pom-pom' from 22.

The smaller resin components are not well defined; great care is required when removing them from the over-large pours, and attention to identifying them with the instruction sheet is necessary to ensure they are located in their correct places on the assembled model.

A photo-etch sheet contains guardwires, ladders, funnel grilles, boat details, breakwater and many other small details – again resulting in a lot of assembly work. The sheet is malleable and hence difficult to work. There is also a small decal sheet containing flags and draught marks, and some lengths of brass wire.

The instructions consist of nine sides of A4 plus a colour sheet showing the camouflage scheme, the colours being identified from the Lifecolor range.

ATLANTIC MODELS

1:700 scale

These two models were originally released by White Ensign Models, and

then re-issued after the UK company ceased trading. According to the boxes, these kits represent *Calcutta* in 1941 and *Coventry* in 1940, but the instructions for *Coventry* include a camouflage scheme for 1941, and the photo-etch sheet in *Calcutta* carries the date 1939 but the camouflage scheme given in the instructions would appear to be correct for 1941.

Apart from these discrepancies, these are both high quality resin kits with distinctly moulded components. They both include detailed photo-etch sheets and the instructions are very well presented. No decals are included.

These two kits are now rarely seen but are worth looking out for.

TRUMPETER

1:700 & 1:350 scales

Trumpeter produce four plastic kits, two at 1:700 scale and two at 1:350 scale. These are of *Colombo* and *Calcutta*.

The 1:700 scale kits are waterline with a one-piece hull and two-piece deck. The box states there are 160+ pieces, and these come

on four different sprues, two of which are duplicated. The four main superstructure components are each supplied on individual sprues. There is a small photo-etch sheet, containing funnel grilles, radar aerials and structural supports for overhanging decks, and a decal sheet containing flags. There is also a rather large name board.

The model of *Calcutta* includes the after HACS, but as she was sunk before this could be fitted, it should be omitted.

Instructions are supplied in a 12-page, A4 booklet, containing ten assembly diagrams. A camouflage scheme is provided for *Colombo* on a colour A4 page, quoting paints from Mr Hobby, Acrysion, Vallejo, Model Master, Tamiya and Humbrol. *Calcutta* is portrayed in light grey overall, with a wooden deck.

The 1:350 scale kits are full-hull, again with the hull in one piece, and the deck and main superstructure parts are similar to those in the smaller version. There are four sprues, one of which is duplicated, and a stand for the model. The photo-etch sheet is larger and includes guardwires, and a length of brass anchor chain is also included. The component count, according to the box, is 290+.

Instructions are supplied in a 16-page A4 landscape booklet containing

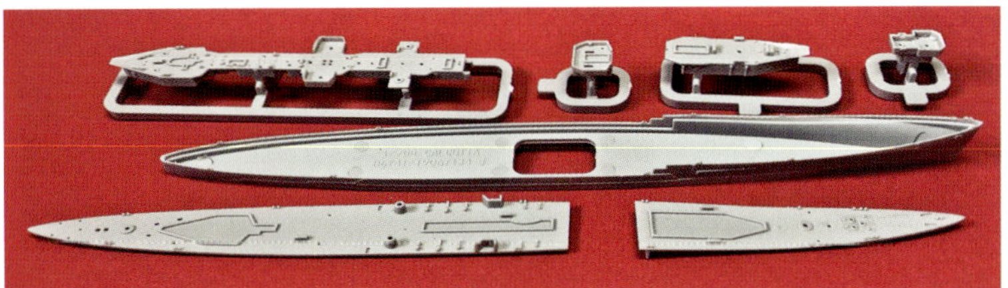

28 assembly diagrams. Colour details are supplied on an A3 sheet, and there is a decal sheet containing flags.

All kits are cleanly moulded in light grey plastic, although the attachment points are rather large and there is some excess plastic (not flash) that needs to be removed, particularly noticeable on the smaller components.

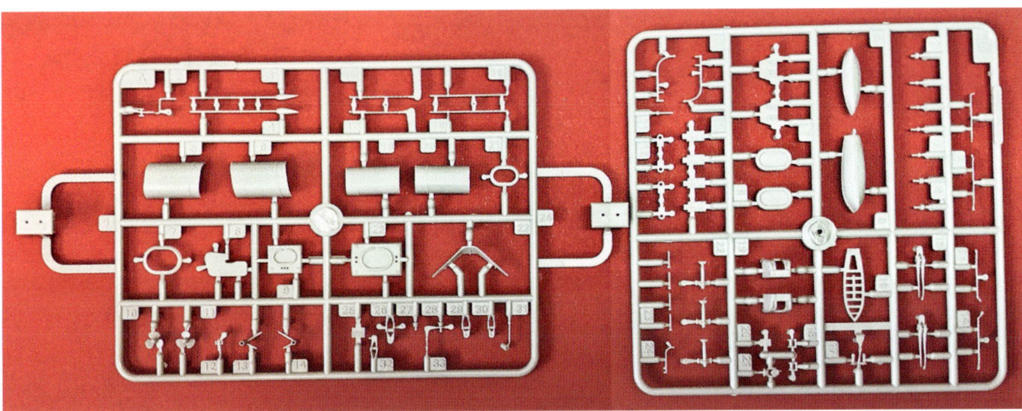

NIKO MODEL

1:700 scale

This kit of ORP *Conrad* represents a 'D' class cruiser, with limited modifications, when operating with the Polish Navy. It could form the basis of a model of *Delhi* but a large number of modifications would be required, the majority of which would be

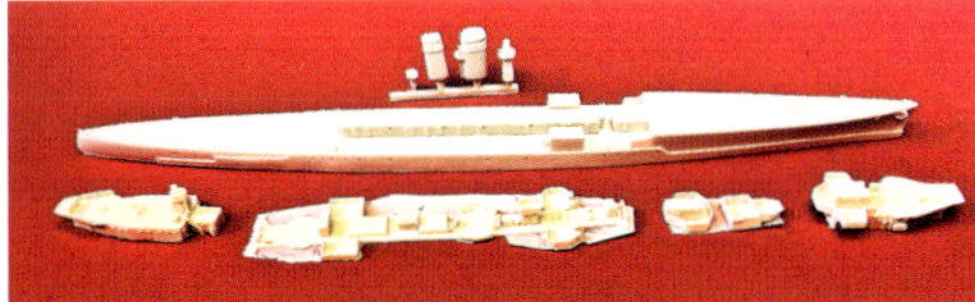

scratch-built, although Black Cat Models of France can supply 3D-printed American equipment.

The kit comprises a waterline resin hull and four plastic bags of finely moulded components. There is a small photo-etch sheet containing funnel grilles, structural

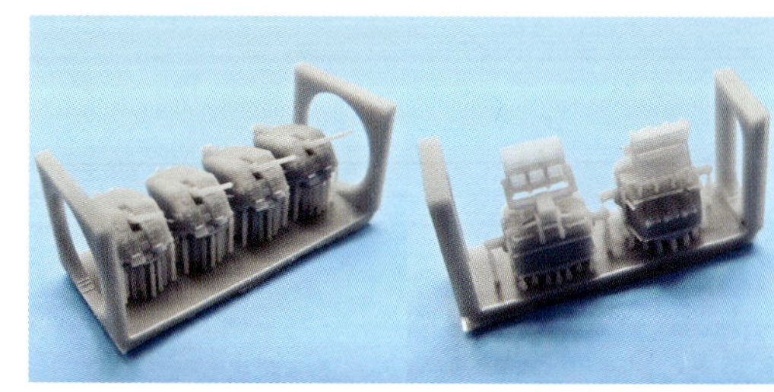

supports for overhanging superstructure, davits, anchor chain and other small details. Instructions are limited to two sheets of A4, an assembly diagram and a general arrangement and painting diagram of *Conrad*.

AJM MODELS

1:700 scale

In addition to the 'C' class cruisers listed earlier, this company produces models of the mercantile conversions *Springbank*, *Alynbank*, *Prince Robert* and *Ulster Queen*. They have also recently released kits of *Palomares* and *Pozarica*, the pair of fruit carriers heavily modified as AA ships.

These are very similar in format to the kits of the cruisers, and the earlier comments apply equally. These kits of unusual subjects are not simple to build but do produce some very pleasing results.

The components of *Alynbank*

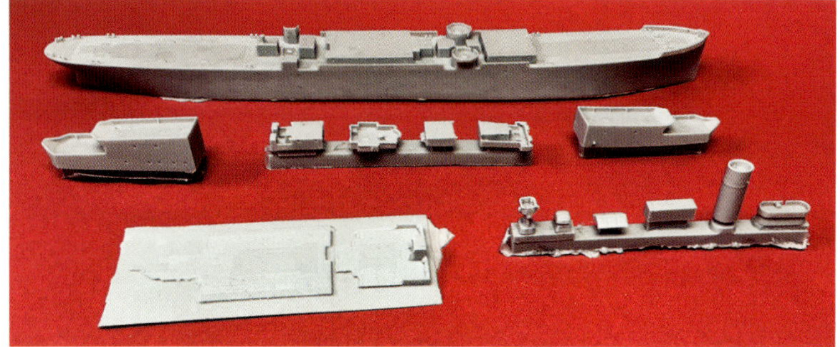

STARLING MODELS

1:700 scale

This Welsh company also produces a kit of *Alynbank*, but it is very different from the AJM offering. The resin parts are cleanly moulded and have much better definition, and the photo-etch sheet is much easier to work with.

The hull does not have superstructure moulded integrally but does have well defined recesses to locate the parts. There are two turned brass masts, but the modeller needs to provide some brass rod. Detailed instructions are contained in an A5 size booklet, which begins by giving

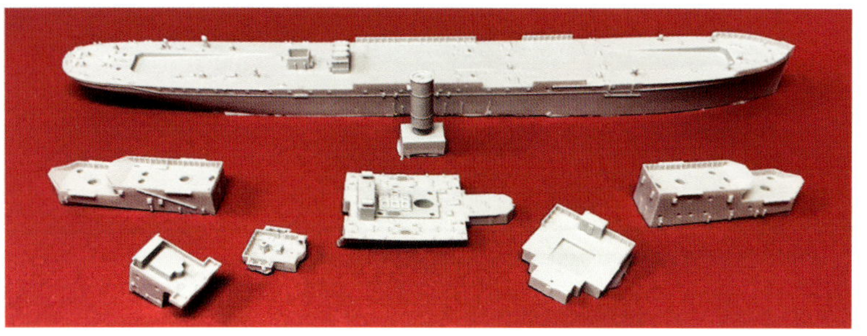

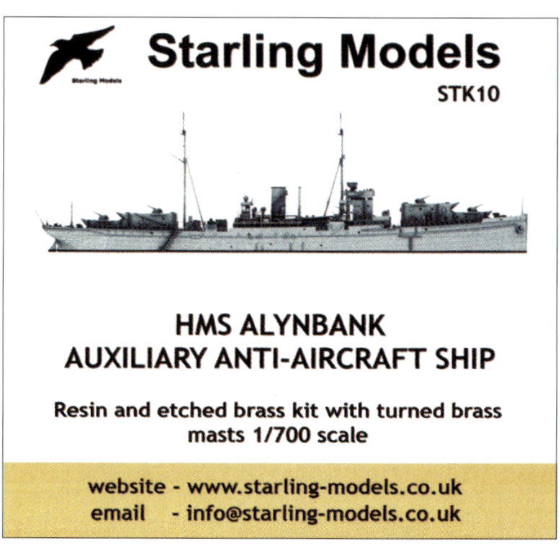

some technical details of the vessel on the front page, and includes both rigging and colour details, just 507c overall.

This kit is much easier to build than the AJM version and illustrates well recent advances in manufacturing techniques.

WSW-MODELLBAU 1:700 scale

This resin kit from Germany of *Scylla* contains finely moulded components, including a waterline hull with the majority of the superstructure moulded integrally. The other components are contained in two plastic bags, the first containing the funnels and other superstructure parts, and the second containing the guns, boats and other small parts.

Instructions come on five sides of A4, the first identifying the components and showing a camouflage pattern for *Scylla* in 1942, and the second containing a general arrangement drawing. The other three sides contain images of the assembly, and identify the size, both length and diameter, of the masts. There is no photo-etch or brass wire.

Although there are only relatively few components, this kit builds into an accurate model, which many will consider to be enhanced by photo-etch guardwires.

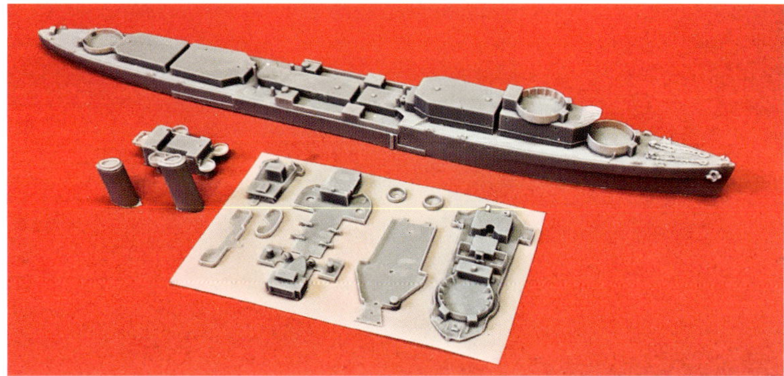

FLYHAWK 1:700 scale

The first thing to notice about this kit of *Naiad* is that one of the box surfaces is a 'blue ocean'. The manufacturer has included this so that it can act as a display base for a waterline model, but it will probably not be used by any serious modeller – and this kit will probably only be tackled by serious modellers!

It can be built either as a waterline or full-hull model, with one-piece above-water and below-water components, a waterline plate and two deck pieces. There is a metal weight that can be fixed to the waterline plate in order to provide a more stable model. The larger superstructure parts are moulded separately and there are just two sprues that are peculiar to this model. The other components are supplied on 'standard' sprues containing weapons and fittings. The very fine masts are supplied on two sprues, contained in a plastic box for protection from damage. There is a photo-etch sheet containing guardrails, ladders,

anchor chain and other small details, and a small decal sheet containing flags.

Instructions are provided on two long, thin, double-sided sheets, not the most convenient format, containing 13 assembly diagrams and colour details of the vessel in 1940. Paint colours are quoted from Mr Hobby and Tamiya, some of which are paint mixes.

This is a very accurate and detailed model, suitable for experienced modellers.

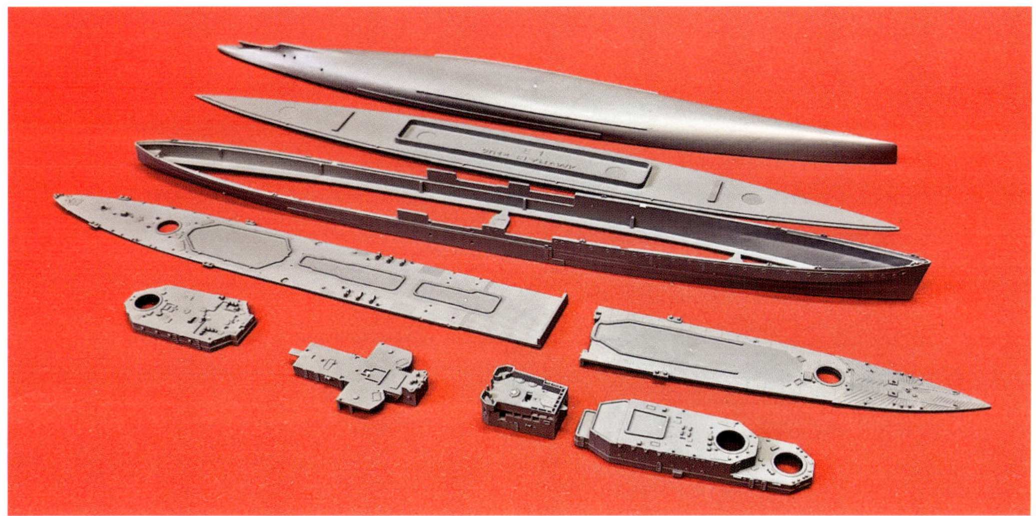

GAGA

1:600 scale

This kit comes from China and is only available on eBay from the seller 'alfa-hobbyuk'. There are no instructions. It is available as either a full-hull or waterline model and contains much fine detail, including guardrails(!), although some of these had been damaged in transport. Despite this fine detail, the deck planking is grossly overscale.

The hull has a significant amount of the superstructure moulded integrally with it. The locations of the separate larger parts of the superstructure are clearly defined by 'pins' on the hull and matching holes in the superstructure. In addition, there are two wafers, one containing the masts, and the

other containing the other details such as gun turrets. The larger parts are cleanly printed, requiring little preparation, but the masts and some of the smaller parts are surrounded by 'printing support pillars', which generally improve the accuracy and quality of the printing, but are difficult to remove without damaging the required part. This is particularly noticeable with the masts where it is often difficult to identify the mast from the 'support pillar'.

This kit is also available at 1:200 scale, when it includes many more components.

No particular vessel is identified but the kit is intended to produce a vessel as designed with five twin 5.25in turrets, which are very nicely printed. Reference drawings of a specific vessel will be a great advantage, if not a necessity.

TRUMPETER

1:350 scale

Trumpeter include three different *Dido* class cruisers in their range, *Argonaut*, *Naiad* and *Scylla*. The first two represent vessels carrying the design armament of five twin 5.25in turrets but the last has the reduced armament of four twin 4.5in mountings, and hence a very different superstructure.

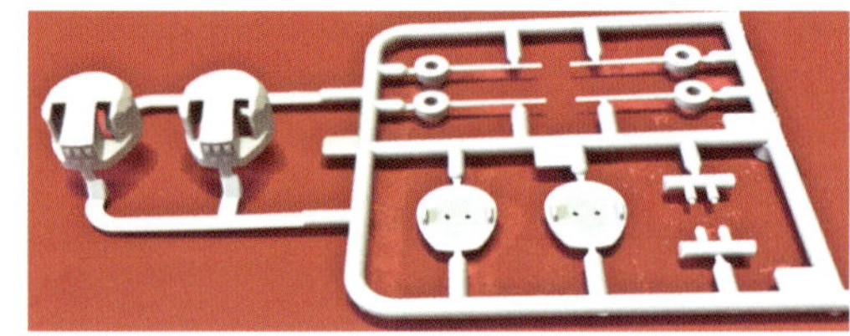

The kit of *Naiad* comprises 600+ pieces (only 520+ for *Scylla*), including a one-piece full-hull moulding. The major parts of *Naiad*'s superstructure come in four separate mouldings, with slightly smaller parts on two sprues (D and E). There are seven different types of sprue, two of which are duplicated (H1 and G), and one (H2) – that with the twin 5.25in gun turrets – is triplicated, giving a 'spare' turret. There are five photo-etch sheets, which include a full set of guardwires as well as other details, and a length of anchor chain. The decal sheet only

contains flags, and there is a stand for the full-hull model.

With *Scylla*, the structures containing the gun mountings are separate from the other main sections (K and V). Sprue G is duplicated and common to all kits, but *Scylla* contains eight different sprues (H4 being quadrupled for the gun mountings), and six photo-etch sheets.

Instructions are contained in a 16-page A4 landscape format booklet, containing 56 assembly diagrams (67 for *Scylla*). There is an A3 colour diagram, that for *Naiad* showing her in a very different camouflage to that in the Flyhawk kit, which was worn later in her career. Paint colours are specified from the Mr Hobby, Acrysion, Vallejo, Model Master, Tamiya and Humbrol ranges.

A very complete kit that can be built into a fine model, particularly if some parts are replaced by items from other manufacturers' detail sets.

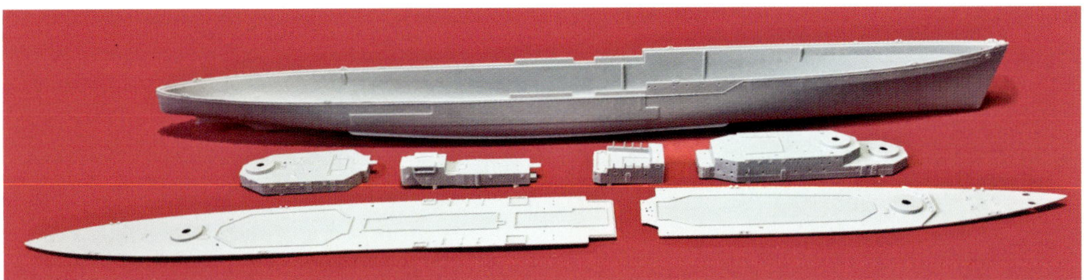

ACCESSORIES

WOOD HUNTER 1:350 scale

From China, Wood Hunter produces a wide range of self-adhesive wooden decks; W35089c being for the Trumpeter 1:350 scale *Calcutta* (05362). The deck is provided in two sections, fore and aft, and contains very clear ruling for the deck planking. Small sections are also provided for the bottoms of the whalers and cabin tops of the cutters. As in peacetime, the decks would have been 'holystoned', the parts on the boats would have been a darker brown than the deck.

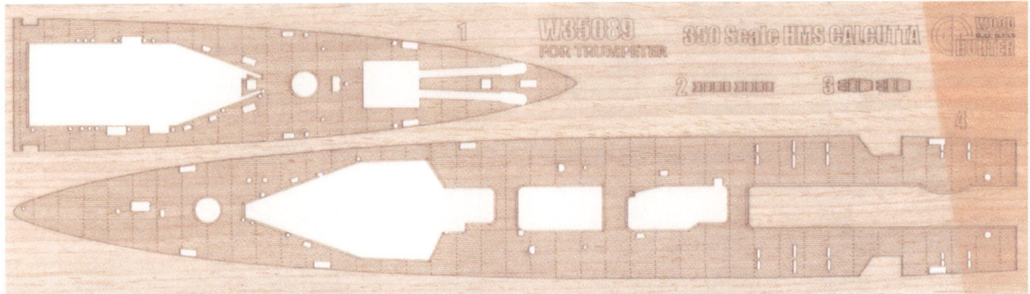

SWORDFISH MODELS NAVAL ACCESSORIES

1:350 scale

The Belgian company of Swordfish Models produces a range of naval accessories from a number of different countries at 1:350, 1:200, 1:144 and 1:72 scales. As well as specific items, such as guns, fire control directors and boats, they also produce generic items, such as ladders, doors, winches and lockers.

In addition, they produce upgrade kits at 1:350 scale, including *Calcutta* 1942, *Colombo* 1943 and *Naiad*.

That for *Calcutta* contains: 5 x 4in Mk XVI guns on Mk XIX mountings, funnels, capstans, cable reels, mushroom vents, 2 x 27ft whalers, 32ft motor cutter, 32ft cutter (all boats are supplied with davits), 9 x carley floats, anchors, 2 x quad Vickers 0.5in MGs, ready-use lockers, Mk III HACS, Mk I pom-pom director, 8 x paravanes, 2 x 36in searchlights, 2 x 20in searchlights, 2 x

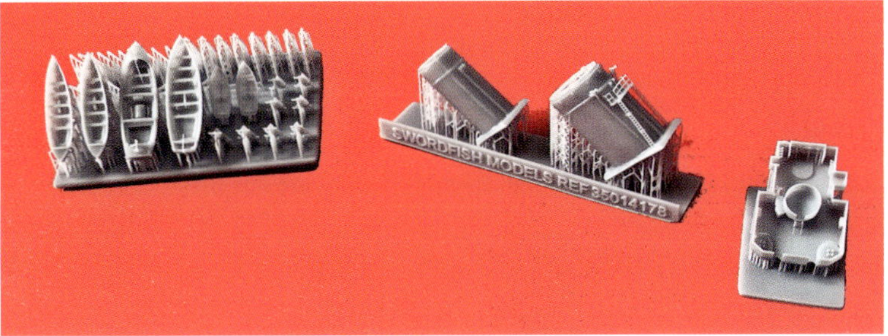
Some of the parts for *Calcutta*

10in searchlights, open bridge, bridge equipment, mast accessories, fore and aft flagstaffs and PE guardwires.

The kit for *Colombo* contains a similar set of parts: 3 x 4in Mk XVI on Mk XIX mountings, funnels, capstans, cable reels, mushroom vents, 2 x 27ft whalers, 32ft motor cutter, 32ft cutter (all boats are supplied with davits), 9 x carley floats, anchors, 2 x twin Bofors Hazemeyer 40mm mounts, 7 x twin 20mm Oerlikon guns on powered Mk V mounts, 2 x 20mm Oerlikon guns, ready-use lockers, Mk IV HACS, RDF aerial antenna, 8 x paravanes, winch, 2 x 10in searchlights, 36in searchlight, bridge equipment, fore superstructures and PE guardwires.

The PE guardwires are for the weather deck only, and include the sheer forward.

Some of the parts for Naiad

The *Naiad* kit contains: 5 x 5.25in QF Mk I dual guns, capstans, cable reels, mushroom vents, 2 x 27ft whalers with davits, 28ft diesel motorboat with crutches, 32ft cutter with crutches, 17 x No 20 carley floats, anchors, 2 x quad 2pdr pom-pom guns, director control tower, 2 x Mk IV rangefinders, 12ft Barr & Stroud rangefinder, 4 x navigation lights, 2 x signalling lamps, winches, bridge and funnels, bridge equipment, 2 x quad Vickers 0.5in Mk II MGs, ready-use lockers, 2 x triple 21in Mk III torpedo tubes, 4 x 44in searchlights, 3 x 20in searchlights, depth charge rail for 6 charges plus reserve charges, 3pdr saluting gun, bollards, window hatches, 12 x smoke floats and 6 x paravanes.

These extensive sets are very high quality and come printed on flat wafers and well-packed in cardboard boxes. Instructions are not included but can be downloaded at no additional cost, and are clear to follow.

YZM MODEL   1:350 scale

This set, *YZ-119*, from China is 3D printed in a black material and is intended for the Trumpeter *Naiad* (05366). It includes ten palettes of printed parts, a very small sheet of photo-etch and some anchor chain. The instructions consist of a single, double-sided sheet showing photographs of five of the palettes, identifying the parts by their equivalent kit part number.

These palettes include replacement funnels, 5.25in gun turrets, boats and carley floats. There is also a replacement deck for kit part E6 and replacement parts for many of the items fitted on it, including the fire control director. Other parts supplied include quadruple pom-poms, torpedo tubes, Oropesa floats and

propellers (for a full-hull model). There are also cable reels, lockers and vents.

Without more detailed instructions, a great deal of research is required to make optimum use of this set. The five turrets are also available separately under the reference *YZ-079*.

BLACK CAT MODELS   1:350 scale

This French company produces a range of accessories at 1:350 scale including the 4in Mk V gun on Mk III mounting and the twin 5.25in turret.

NNT MODELL   1:700 scale

This German firm produces some fine 3D printed twin 4.5in QF Mk III UD Mountings (x4), product number: 3DModelB703, at 1:700 scale.

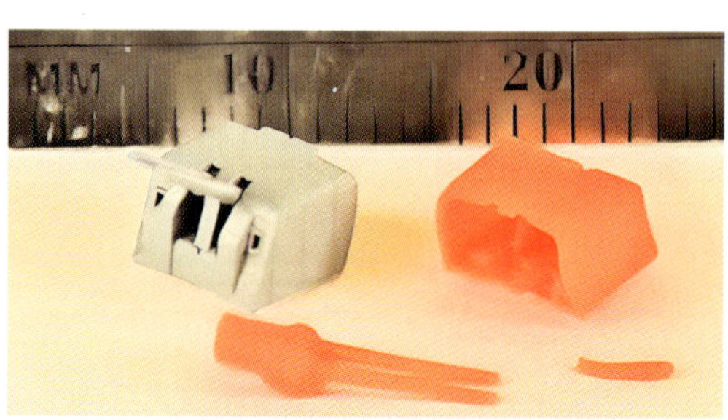

Modelmakers' Showcase

TRUMPETER *CALCUTTA* 1:350 scale   By ROB MATTHEWS

HMS *Calcutta* is depicted in her 'Alexandria' camouflage scheme. It Is the Trumpeter model in 1:350 scale built 'out of the box' (OOB) with the weapons, HACs and ship's boats being replaced by Micro Master 3D printed items. The quad 2pdr and the rafts are from Black Cat models, and the figures are from North Star. The deck is aftermarket wood and she is finished in Sovereign Colourcoat paints. The fit of the Trumpeter kit was flawless.

HMS Calcutta
C-Class AA Cruiser
Mediterranean, April 1941

TRUMPETER *COLOMBO* 1:350 scale

By ROB MATTHEWS

HMS *Colombo* was built from the 1:350 Trumpeter kit. Construction was straight-forward and fit excellent. Ship's boats, 4in guns, ammunition lockers, twin Oerlikons, HACs and 271 Radar housing are all Micro Master 3D printed replacements. The twin Bofors and rafts are from Black Cat Models. The etched railings are from Flyhawk and previous Trumpeter models.

Figures are a mixture of Black Cat Models and North Star. It was pointed out post-build that *Colombo* almost certainly did not have forward radial davits as depicted here but instead used quadrantal along with *Carlisle* and *Caledon*. In addition, she *may* have had a Mk III gunnery director with Yagi aerials in the position of the top aft twin Oerlikon. Original photographs are unclear.

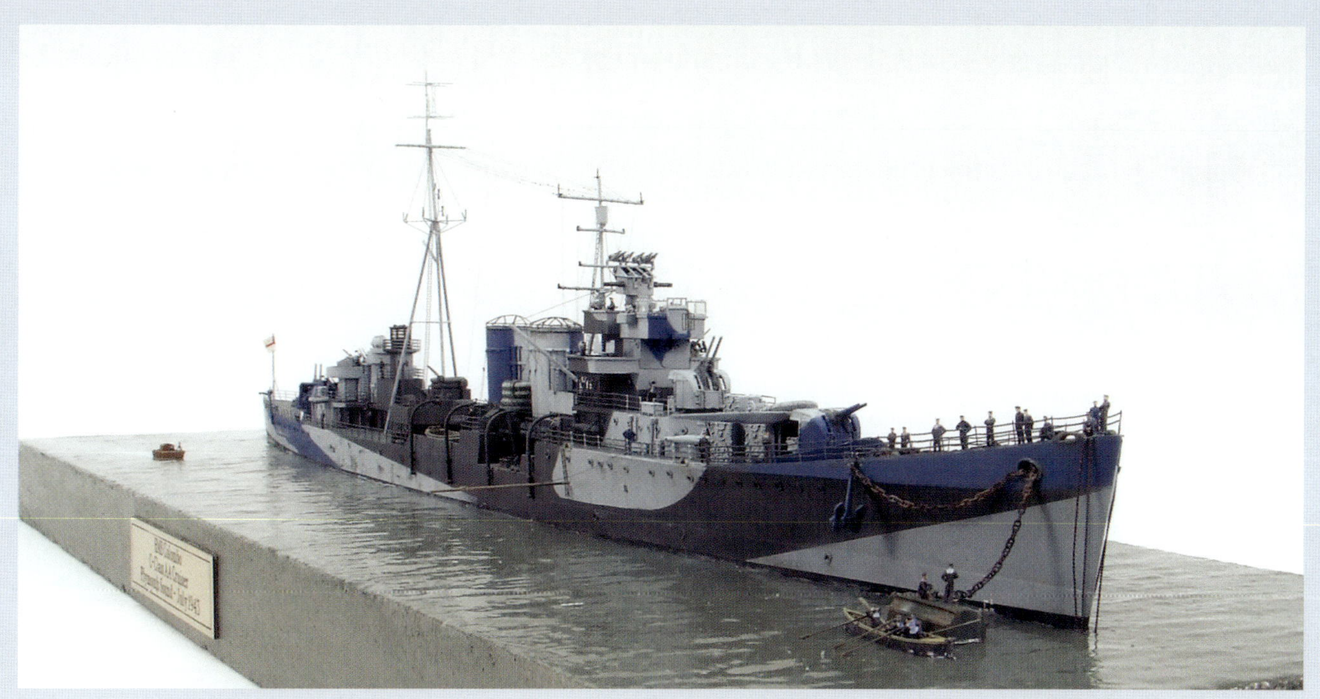

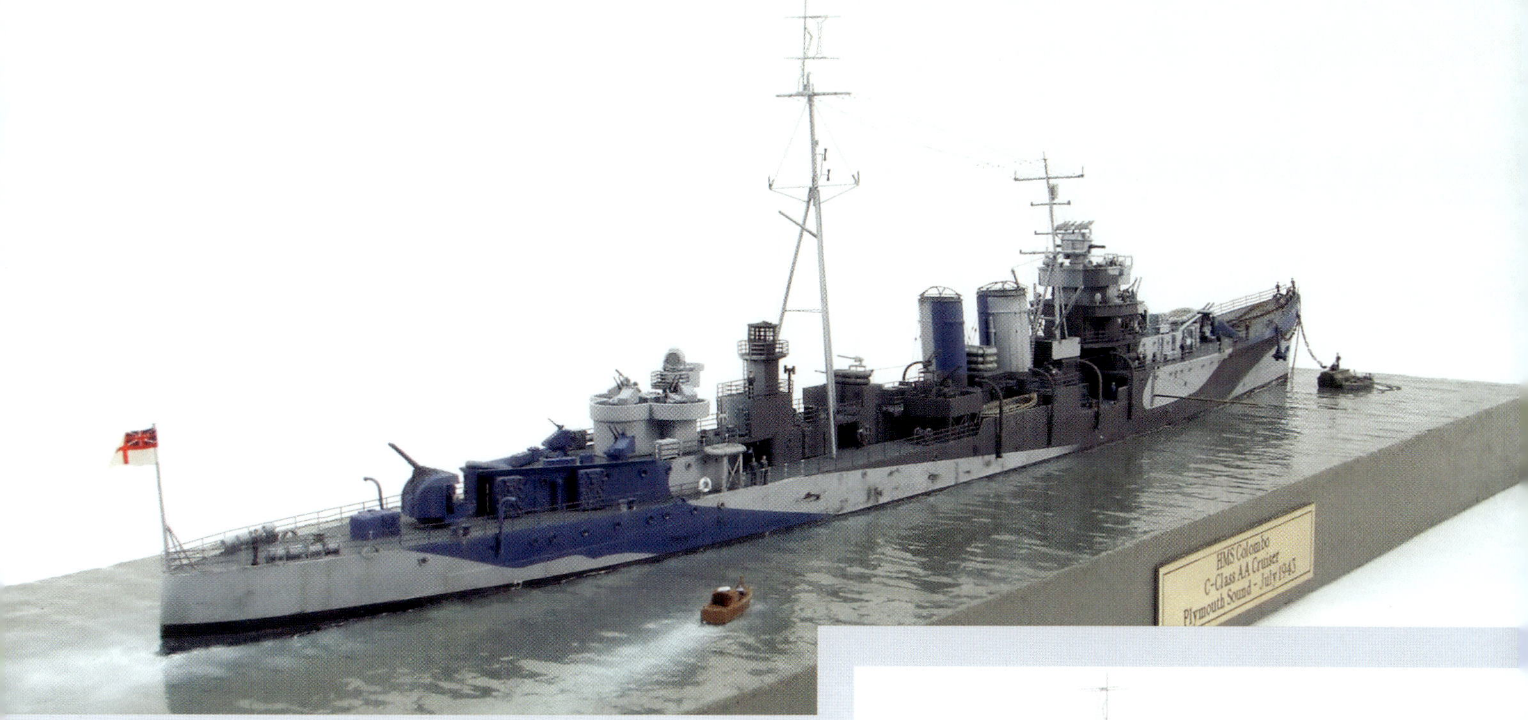
HMS Colombo
C-Class AA Cruiser
Plymouth Sound - July 1943

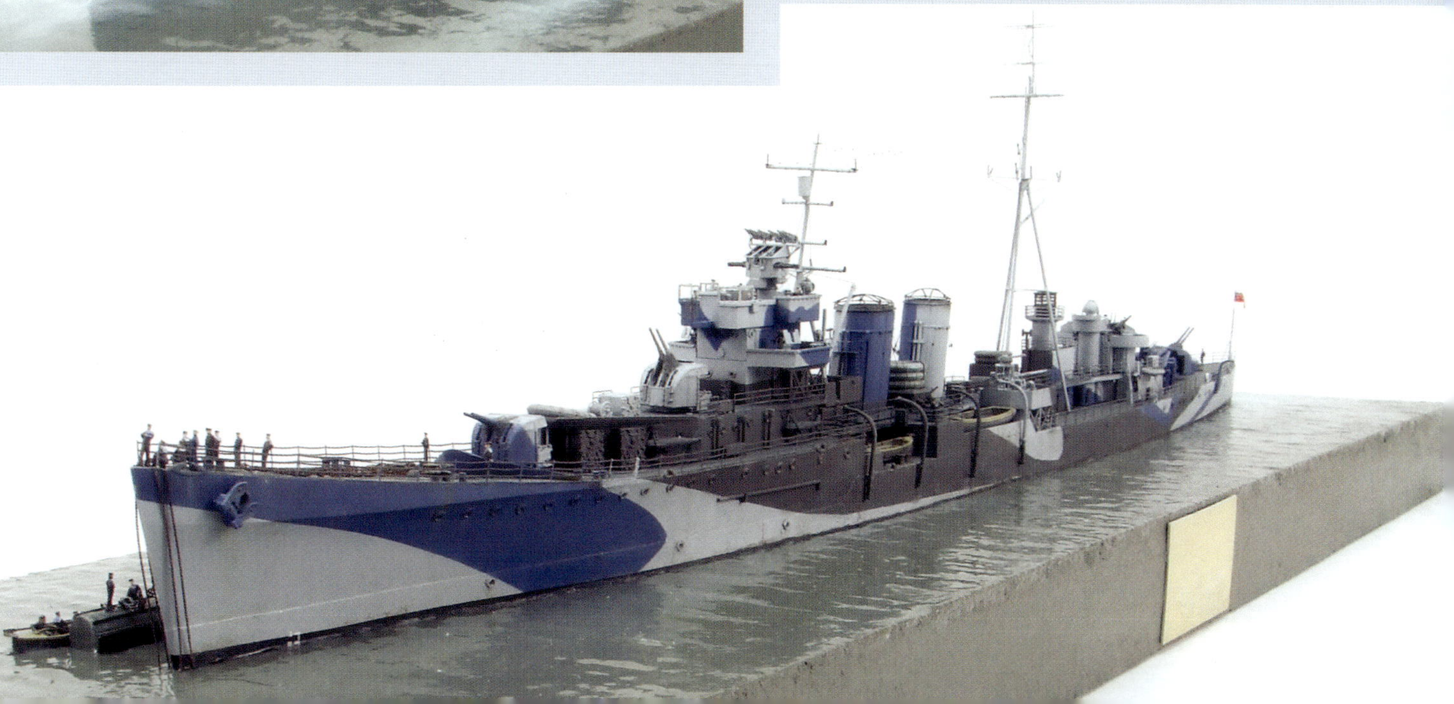

AJM MODELS *SPRINGBANK* AND *ALYNBANK*
1:700 scale
By ROGER J C THOMAS

At first glance, these two models of converted Bank Line anti-aircraft ships, by the Polish firm AJM Models, look almost identical; however, there are marked differences in these two sister ships. The model of HMS *Springbank* represents the appearance of the ship, while escorting convoy HG73, shortly before she was sunk by *U-201* on the night of 27 September 1941. HMS *Alynbank* has a camouflage scheme as worn in 1943, while operating off Sicily. The most obvious difference between the two ships was the catapult and Fairey Fulmar fitted amidships on *Springbank*. The kits are not straightforward to build, as they require a great deal of care and patience; the resin is brittle, which also suffers from some warping in places, there are large numbers of very small parts attached to thick pouring blocks, which are not numbered and, consequently, are difficult to identify. The extensive photo-etch is

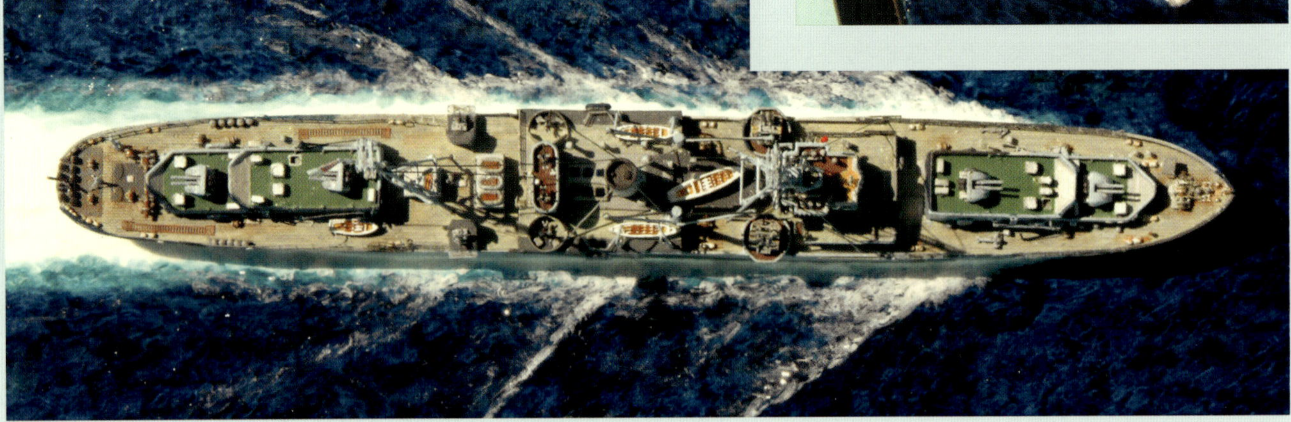

very fine and soft, which results in considerable care being needed to avoid unwanted distortion when cutting and folding. The instructions only show completed assemblies, with no clear distinction between resin and photo-etched parts, and suffer from no folding directions. Although both kits are challenging and are only suitable for experienced modellers, they nevertheless do produce very interesting models of unusual ships that are unlikely ever to appear in plastic.

STARLING MODELS *ALYNBANK* (1942) 1:700 scale   By ROGER J C THOMAS

This model of HMS *Alynbank* was built straight out of the box, using the photo-etched brass supplied with the kit. Construction was relatively straightforward and was guided by the excellent coloured sub-assembly drawings in the instructions. No additional 3D printed parts or scratch-building was necessary, apart from a small quantity of brass rod, used for the yardarms, stanchions, booms, and to support the supplied turned brass masts. I used carefully selected lengths of shed cat's whiskers for the rigging, as it is stiff and holds its shape well (NB no cats suffered during the construction of this model). The ship is shown as she appeared in 1942 escorting convoys in Atlantic waters, with five ship's boats amidships, and a searchlight tower abaft the funnel. This arrangement was changed in 1943, when two of the boats and the searchlights were landed, and were replaced by four single 20mm Oerlikon cannons; as can be found in the AJM Models kit. The sea base was built up with layers of Daler-Rowney acrylic gesso and texture paste, applied using a palate knife and paint brushes of different sizes; before being painted with a mix of children's poster paint, and finished using AK Atlantic blue water gel.

WSW *SCYLLA* 1:700 scale

By JIM BAUMANN

Despite WW2 being a little late for my sphere of interest, I have always been attracted to the bright blue camouflage scheme on the box-lid of the WSW 1/700 resin kit, which had resided in my stash for around 5 years... Unfortunately the blue proved erroneous!

I had hoped for a short sharp build, but as ever this model was destined to be full of trials and some tribulations!

Part of the fundamental problem was that it would appear that WSW mastered the kit based exclusively on the *Profile Morskie* plans, which upon further examination of high resolution photos and other drawings were rather flawed...!

Some of the inaccuracies that I cured were wrong porthole placement, solid bridge top, incorrect splinter shield heights, shapes and disposition, removal of break-

waters that were not present on the real ship, deck shapes and surface being incorrect, funnel tops wrong, missing aft blast shield as well as many other tiny problems.

But perhaps the most obvious and serious mistake was my own fault! Having checked numerous internet sources as well as books such as *Cruisers in Camera*, I chose to believe the often cited port-side camouflage attributed to *Scylla* to be correct – the same pattern that was shown and captioned in photos in the *Profile Morskie* – but as I found out a long way into the build is actually that of her near-sister HMS *Charybidis*. Fortunately, I had to hand a high-quality starboard side view,

which showed the subtleties of the scheme very well!

I was too far along with the build to contemplate stripping paint and detail and as all my 1:700 models reside in wall-mounted display cases, with starboard side showing, I decided to live with the flaw and learn from my misadventure!

TRUMPETER *EURYALUS* 1:350 scale   By ROB MATTHEWS

HMS *Euryalus* modelled in her garish early war garb uses the Trumpeter HMS *Naiad* as its base kit. A degaussing line around the whole hull had to be whittled off and the difference between the two vessels then consisted largely of Carley float placement. Fitting the superstructure pieces to the deck was 'tight' and once again involved some extensive whittling.

All of the main guns, ship's boats, HACs, torpedo tubes, vents and many fittings throughout were replaced with Micro Master products. They provide state of the art 3D printed pieces that bring unprecedented detail to scale ship modelling.

The whole upper bridge structure was replaced with a 'drop-in' offering from Swordfish Models, removing the headache of bending photo-etch ladders and platforms! That said, the photo-etch provided with the kit was extensive and very satisfactory.

The quad pom-poms, Carley floats and figures were courtesy of Black Cat Models as was the excellent 3D printed Harbour Defence Motor Launch that is depicted motoring up to check its charge.

Rigging was done with Infini 20/40 gauge lycra line with odd bits supplemented by Modelkasten metal wire.

Painting was done exclusively with Resolution Colourcoat enamels that provide wonderfully authentic WW2 Royal Navy colours.

I hope the whole ensemble does justice to this iconic WW2 cruiser.

HMS Euryalus
Dido Class Cruiser
Home waters – June 1941

TRUMPETER *NAIAD* 1:350 scale

By STEVE HEWITT

This is Trumpeter's 1:350 HMS *Naiad* built with the addition of the YZM Model 3D print detail set. The base kit, being a relatively new release from 2024, is a cleanly moulded and generally accurate representation of this first batch *Dido* class cruiser, being very close to published dimensions in length and beam. The detail parts are quite well done within the limitations of injection moulding, with several frets of photo etch to enhance these in some areas. The kit is moulded as a one-piece, full hull, with integral strakes and a nicely moulded (accurate for *Naiad*) degaussing coil. The only issues encountered in assembly were the tight fit of the deckhouses onto their location ribs and the generally undersized location holes for the deck details. Both problems were easily solved with test fitting and trimming/drilling.

The tripod masts are provided in plastic and are just robust enough when built to take the strain of rigging, but some may wish to replace these structures with brass or nickel rod of the appropriate gauge for added strength.

The 3D printed detail set from YZM models takes the model to another level, with a complete open bridge, armament including the 5.25in main turrets, pompoms and quad Vickers guns, torpedo tubes and many other deck details. They are all far superior to the kit parts and well worth adding to the model. They are all printed with very fine detail and are provided on

fine supports with protective cages. The instructions simply refer to the kit part numbers for which the 3D prints are direct replacements. Apart from increased detail and accuracy, the 3D parts simplify and speed-up assembly considerably.

FLYHAWK *NAIAD* 1:700 scale

By DAVE EYLES

Flyhawk are renowned for the level of research that goes into each of their models, and so when models are built straight from the box, as this one is, the modeller can be confident in its accuracy. The quality and fidelity of manufacture are second to none, and so there is little (if any) need to replace parts with those of 3D printing manufacture, although Flyhawk have supplied a few of such parts in their latest kits.

The only variation from the instructions in this model was the colours of the camouflage scheme, as the one given in the instructions was only worn for a short time.

HMS *Coventry* 1940

HMS *Calcutta* 1941

HMS *Coventry* 1941

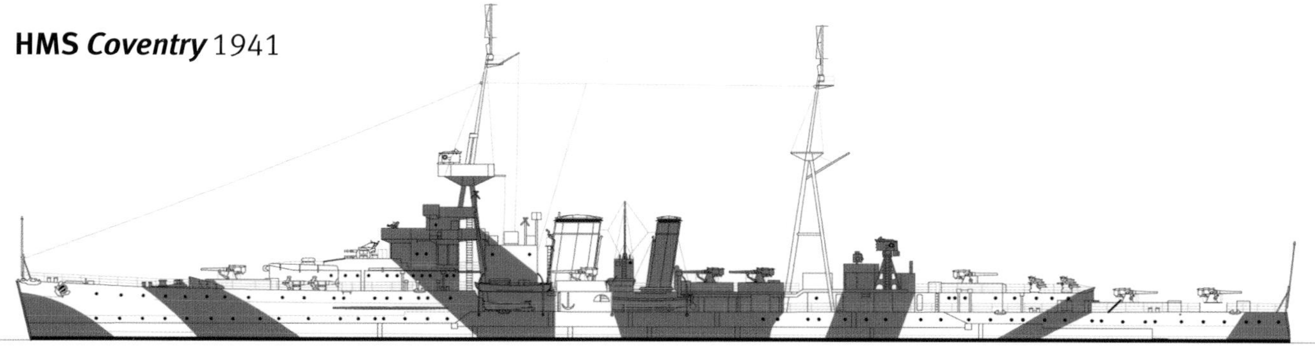

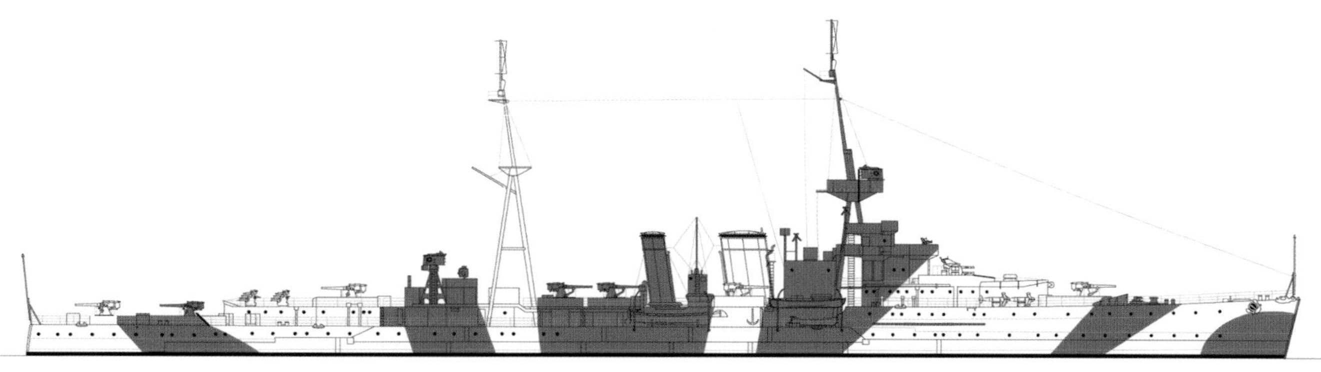

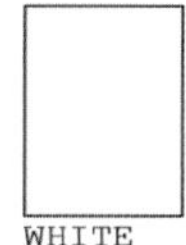

HMS *Delhi* 1942

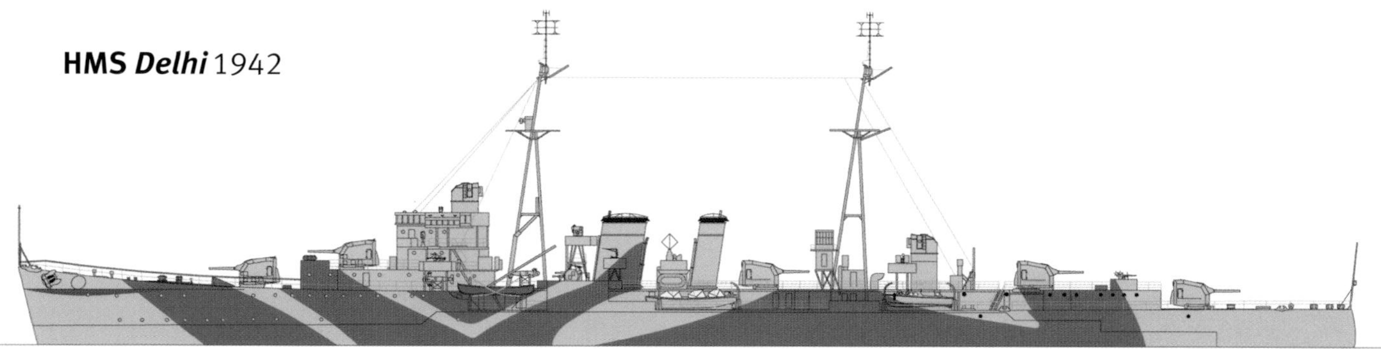

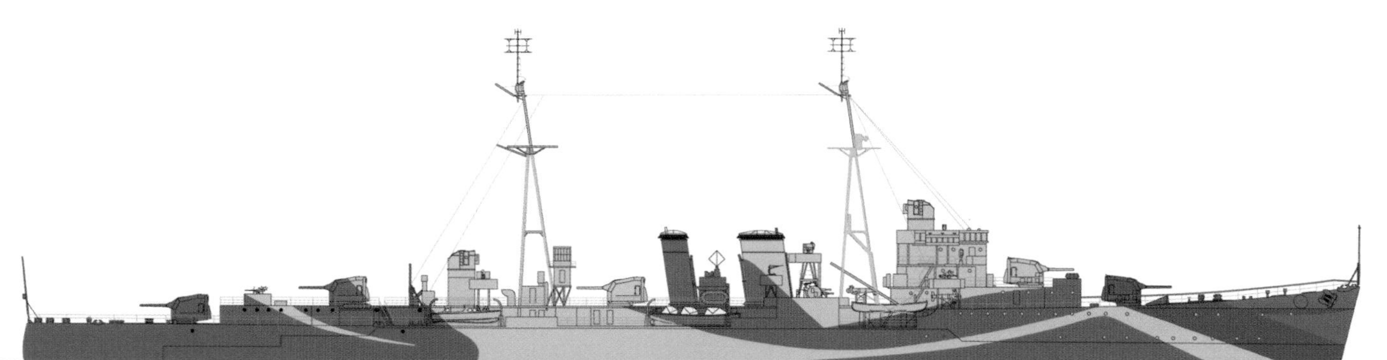

HMS *Delhi* 1943

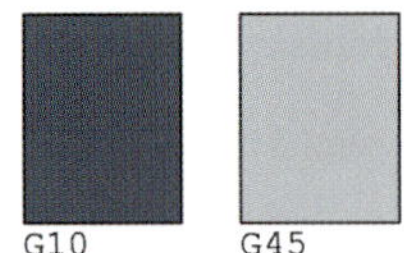

HMS *Alynbank* 1940

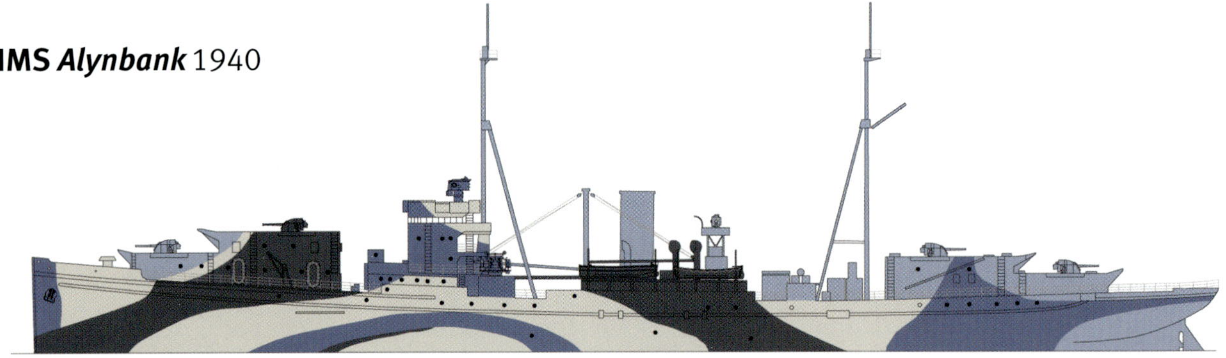

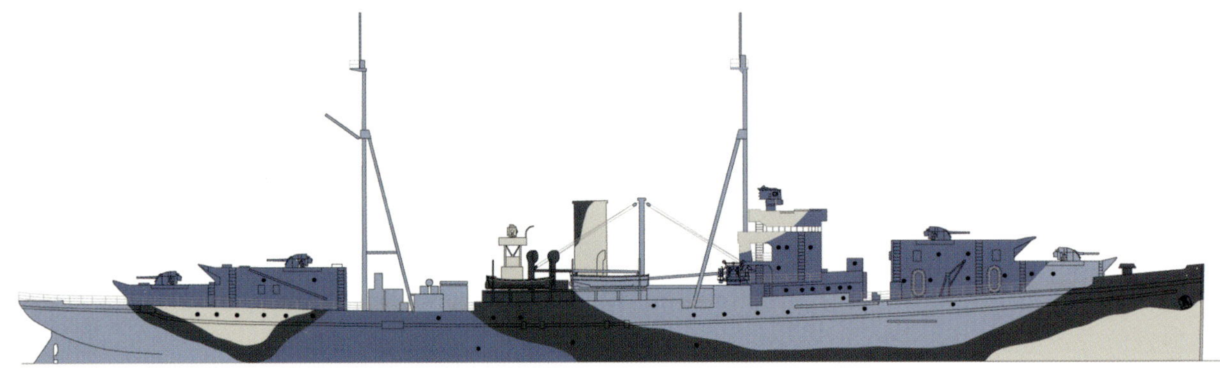

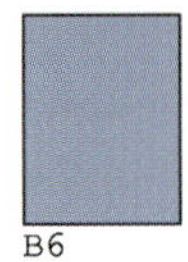

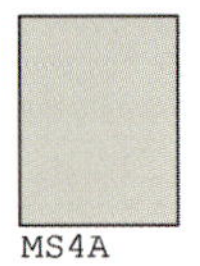

HMCS *Prince Robert* 1943

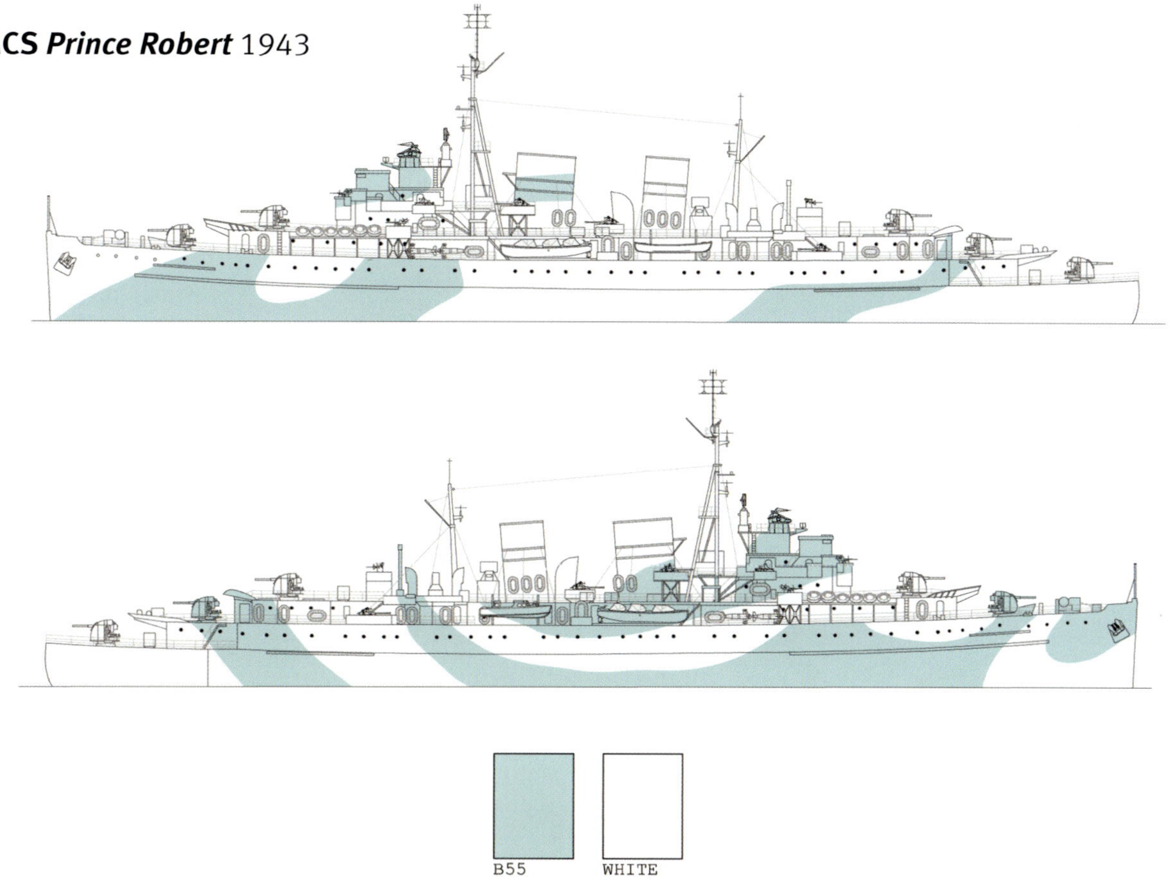

HMCS *Prince Robert* 1945

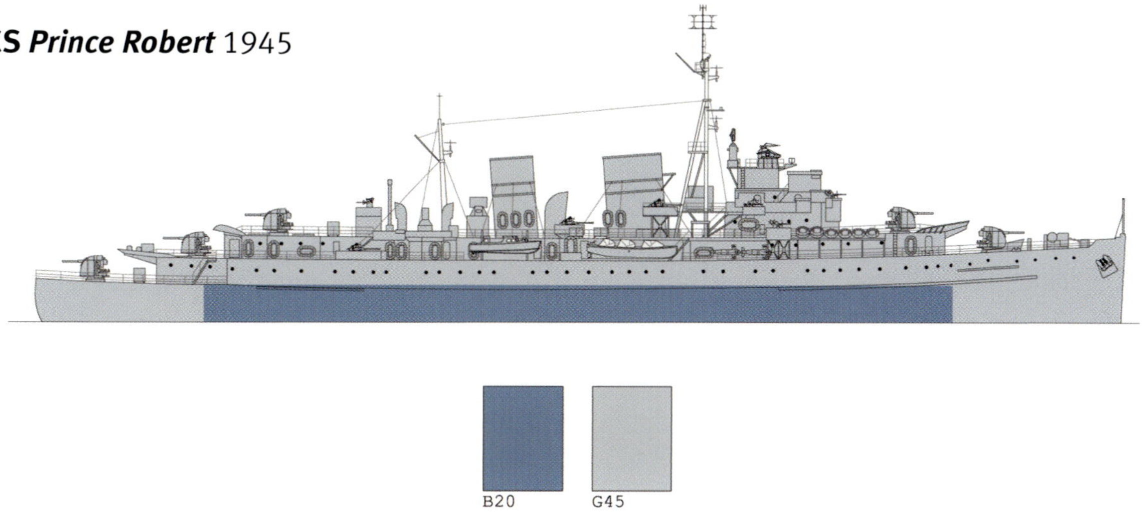

B55 WHITE

B20 G45

HMS *Naiad* 1942

507B 507B

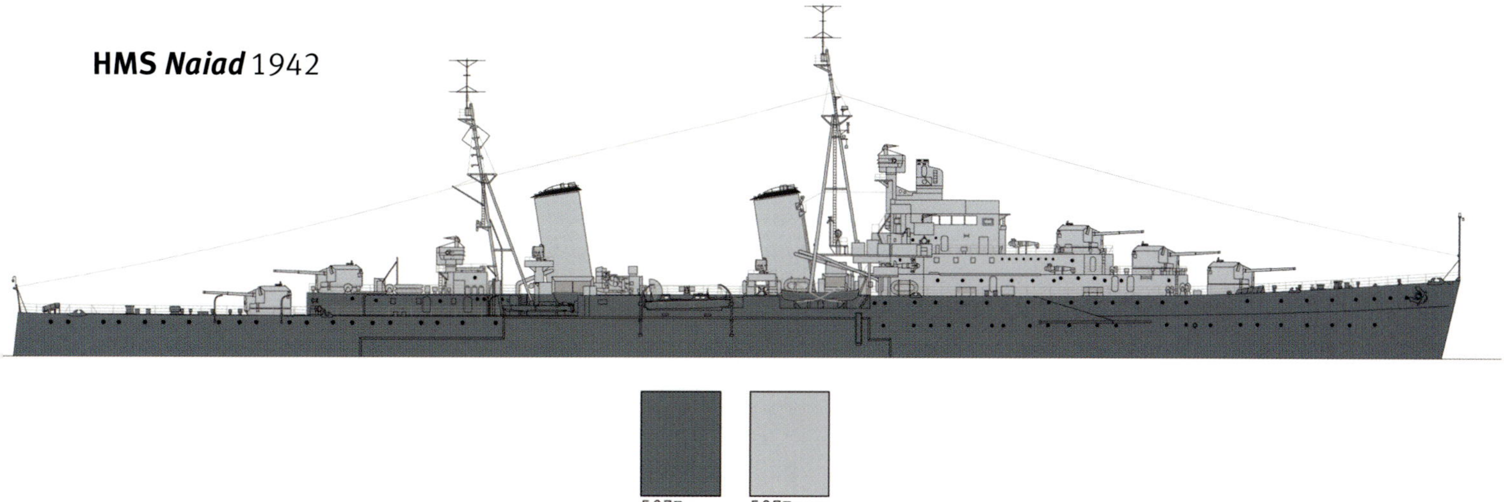

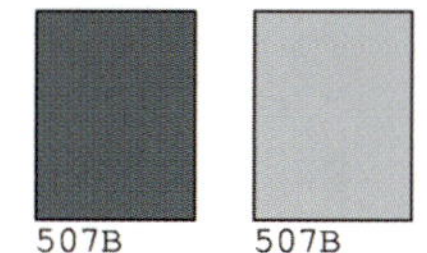

HMS *Scylla* 1942

HMS *Black Prince* 1943

DIDO CLASS CRUISERS

Throughout the inter-war years, the Admiralty struggled to afford the number of cruisers needed to protect the world's largest merchant fleet and to police its extensive overseas empire. In an attempt to keep down the size and firepower of the Royal Navy's likely opponents, the British negotiated a series of treaties that came to dominate cruiser design. These developments have been covered in previous ShipCraft titles: the 8in-armed heavy cruisers of the Washington Treaty era (*ie* the 'County' class, see ShipCraft 19); the 6in cruisers of the 1930 London Treaty (see ShipCraft 31); and their larger successors (*ie* the 'Town' and 'Colony' classes, see ShipCraft 33). By the mid-1930s the main armament of all British cruisers – even the largest – was standardised on the 6in gun, but by the time a new class of small cruiser for fleet duties was being designed the international situation had prompted consideration of improved AA defence.

The conversions of *Curlew* and *Coventry* as prototype AA ships during the Abyssinian Crisis of 1935–36 (see above) were considered a step in the right direction. These vessels had been fitted with 4in guns, as was standard heavy AA armament for the majority of cruisers, but for the new design, it was felt that a larger calibre of gun was required for surface action. The twin 5.25in gun mounting was already in production for the secondary armament of the *King George V* class battleships, and so this was chosen, giving the new class a nominally 'dual-purpose' main armament, even though it was detrimental to pure AA performance.

To reduce the time for the design and construction of the vessels, the hull and scantlings were based on the *Arethusa* class, and the machinery installation was similar, although the cruising turbine was omitted. With all the armament being in turrets, it was possible to place the mountings closer together without worrying about the blast of a gun affecting the crew of nearby mountings. The *Arethusa* class had carried ten guns (6 x 6in and 4 x 4in), so to match this, it was necessary to mount five twin 5.25in turrets. This was achieved by placing three forward, superfiring over each other, and two aft, designated 'A', 'B', 'Q', 'X' and 'Y' from bow to stern, resulting in a tall and distinctive profile.

Initial requirements included two quadruple 0.5in machine gun mounts, two triple 21in torpedo tubes and aircraft facilities. Approval of the design in 1936 removed the aircraft facilities and added two quadruple pom-pom mounts. Machinery was on the unit principle, with three-drum small tube boilers. These operated at 400psi, considerably higher than previous classes, and produced 58,000shp, later increased to 62,000shp when the design beam was increased by 6in to main-

tain stability, for a maximum speed of 32 knots (later 32½ knots) at standard displacement. The range was just 5500nm at 16 knots, sufficient for a fleet cruiser.

Armour was 3in non-cemented on the sides of the machinery and magazines, and on deck over the magazine crowns. Elsewhere, it was 1in, type 'D'.

The twin 5.25in mounting was originally to be the Mark I but this was replaced by a long trunk Mark II, which improved ammunition supply and reduced the handling crew, which eased congestion in the accommodation. The barrels of these mountings could be elevated independently. A single Mk IV DCT was fitted at the rear of the bridge, with two HACSs, one forward and one aft. Pole masts were replaced by tripods to reduce 'wooding' and the funnels were raked to minimise smoke interference with the DCT. All boats were carried on davits so that no boat crane was required, one of the many weight-saving measures included.

Eventually, all the 5.25in turrets were fitted with remote power control to enable them to follow the HA DCTs in both training and elevation.

The vessels were lightly constructed to reduce the displacement, and early experience in bad weather revealed problems requiring additional stiffening, particularly forward. Problems included turrets jamming and leaking, but with the modifications and experience in operation, the ships proved very successful.

The first five ships were ordered in the 1936 Programme. The 1937 Programme contained two more, and three more in the 1938 Programme. With the outbreak of war, three more were contained in the 1939 Programme, and another three in the Emergency 1939 Programme. A total of sixteen ships were ordered to the original design, although the last five were

This view of 'A', 'B' and 'Q' turrets of *Dido* clearly shows the imposing profile of this class.

constructed to a modified design, often referred to as the *Bellona* class. Because of equipment supply shortages, only a limited number of vessels could be completed as designed.

Bonaventure was built by Scotts Shipbuilding and Engineering Company at Greenock, and was the first of the class to be commissioned on 24 May 1940, having been launched on 19 April 1939.

Production difficulties with the turrets forced the navy to substitute a 4in Mk V star-shell gun for 'X' turret on *Bonaventure*, and this was not replaced before she was lost. For close-in protection, the two quadruple 2pdr pom-pom mountings were positioned just forward of the aft funnel, one on each side, and these were backed-up by two quadruple Vickers 0.50in machine gun mounts on the bridge wings, as designed.

Bonaventure was equipped with a Type 279 metric air warning radar, with separate Transmitting and Receiving antennas at the masthead, and it was intended she be fitted with a Type 128A asdic, but none was available when she was completing. On trials *Bonaventure* had a mean displacement of 6400 tons, achieving 30.46 knots on 63,000shp. Standard design displacement was 5450 tons.

Bonaventure joined the Mediterranean Fleet on 29 March 1941, the day after the Battle of Matapan. The cruiser was ordered to join the escort of Convoy GA 8 which was bound for Alexandria and, at about 0255 on the 31st, while south of Crete, she was hit amidships on the starboard side by two torpedoes fired by the Italian submarine *Ambra*. One torpedo struck at the aft end of the forward engine room and the other detonated abreast the aft engine room, destroying the watertight bulkhead and exposing 'X' magazine to the open sea. The flooding caused a severe list to starboard and, within six minutes, she capsized with the loss of 139 of her crew. The 310 survivors were rescued by *Hereward* and the Australian destroyer *Stuart*. *Bonaventure* was the largest warship sunk by an Italian submarine in World War II.

Naiad was the second vessel to commission, on 24 July 1940. She was built by Hawthorn Leslie and Company at Hebburn-on-Tyne, and had been launched on 3 February 1939. She completed with the full armament as designed and with radar Type 279, but the asdic Type 128A was still unavailable. Her standard displacement was 5574 tons. By January 1942, the two 0.5in mountings had been replaced by five single 20mm mountings.

Between February and March 1941 she was under repair for weather damage suffered while serving in northern waters, the strengthening increasing her displacement to 5699 tons. Transferred to the Mediterranean, in March 1942 she sailed from Alexandria to attack an Italian cruiser that had been reported damaged. This report was false, but, whilst making her return, on 11 March 1942 *Naiad* was sunk by the German submarine *U-565* south of Crete; 77 of her ship's company were lost.

Dido. The name-ship of the class was built by Cammell Laird Shipyard of Birkenhead, being launched on 18 July 1939 and commissioned on 30 September 1940 at Birkenhead, the third of the class to do so.

She was completed with four twin 5.25in turrets in 'A', 'B', 'X' and 'Y' positions with a 4in Mk V star-shell gun in 'Q' position, her standard displacement being 5600 tons. The 4in and the machine guns were removed in the latter half of 1941 at the Brooklyn Navy Yard, USA, when the 'Q' position 5.25in turret was shipped and five single 20mm guns were fitted, two of which replaced the original quadruple 0.5in machine guns. 'B' turret was completely refurbished.

Dido was fitted with a Type 281 metric air warning radar, with separate Tx/Rx antennas, in lieu of the Type 279 fitted to *Bonaventure*, *Naiad* and *Phoebe*. Her degaussing coil was fitted externally, *Dido* and *Naiad* being the only ones in the class to have this feature, as all the others were internal.

In 1943 two more single 20mm guns were added and in 1944 four twin 20mm, two of which replaced single guns. The radar outfit was altered by the addition of a Type 272 centimetric target indication radar, carried in distinctive protective perspex 'lantern', a Type 284 main armament ranging and splash-spotting radar, two Type 285 ranging sets for anti-aircraft fire control, with six element Yagi antenna with separate Tx/Rx, and two Type 282 centimetric ranging sets with twin Yagi antennas.

An April 1944 lists show *Dido* only carried eight 20mm guns at that time. *Dido* had cross-bracing between the after legs of the foremast, not carried by others in the class.

Dido survived the war, retaining all five twin 5.25in turrets, and in July 1945 took King George VI and Queen Elizabeth to the Isle of Man. In 1953, as flagship of the Reserve Fleet, she took part in the Fleet Review to celebrate the Coronation of Queen Elizabeth II. She was decommissioned and sold for scrap to Thomas W Ward, being broken up at Barrow-in-Furness in 1957.

Phoebe was built by Fairfield Shipbuilding

Naiad in 1941 with her armament as designed. Note the elaborate camouflage scheme.

and Engineering Company, Govan, being launched on 25 March 1939, and commissioned on the same day as *Dido*. She completed with four twin 5.25in turrets and was fitted with a 4in star-shell gun in 'Q' position forward of the bridge. Her displacement was slightly lower than that of *Dido* at 5580 tons. The star-shell gun was removed during her refit between November 1941 and April 1942 at Brooklyn Navy Yard, New York, after being torpedoed during an Italian air attack off Bardia in August 1941. The quadruple 0.5in machine guns were also removed, and a quadruple 2pdr pom-pom mounting replaced the star-shell gun, to reduce topweight. Five single 20mm guns were also fitted. On return to Plymouth, the original radar Type 279 was replaced by Type 281, and ranging radars Type 284 and 285 were added.

In October 1942, whilst on passage to Freetown, *Phoebe* was hit on the port side abreast 'Q' turret forward by a torpedo fired by *U161*. She sustained major structural damage and flooding, with all forward turrets unusable. In January 1943, she returned to the Brooklyn Navy Yard for repair, and then to Vickers Armstrong shipyard at Barrow in Furness in July.

A replacement 'A' turret was fitted and ranging radar was installed for the HA mountings, together with surface warning radar Type 272 and IFF interrogation outfits. Six more 20mm guns were added. During these repairs in early 1943, two quadruple 40mm Bofors guns replaced the 2pdr pom-pom mounts, and six twin and four single 20mm guns were added.

After VJ-Day, *Phoebe* returned home for refitting and spent five years in the Mediterranean Fleet. In early 1948, she assisted in the British withdrawal from Mandatory Palestine, embarking the last GOC Palestine and rearguard troops, as the evacuation was completed. After a period in reserve, she was sold to BISCO in 1956 for demolition by Hughes Bolckow at Blyth where she arrived in tow on 1 August the same year.

Hermione was built by Alexander Stephen and Sons, Glasgow, Yard number 560, being launched on 18 May 1939 and commissioned on 25 March 1941. When completed her armament was as designed with five twin 5.25in turrets but in

Phoebe in 1943, with 'A' turret missing and US 40mm Bofors guns replacing the 2pdr pom-poms.

October–November 1941, the 0.5in machine guns were replaced by five single Oerlikon 20mm cannon at Gibraltar. *Hermione* was fitted with Type 281 radar and had ranging set Type 285 fitted to the HA DCTs.

Hermione was part of *Force A* which escorted supply convoy MW 11, from Alexandria to Malta in Operation Vigorous. On 14 and 15 June 1942, *Hermione* expended most of her ammunition while defending the ships against heavy air attacks and had to return to Alexandria. On 15 June, at 0019 hours, *U-205* fired a spread of three torpedoes hitting *Hermione* on the starboard side. The ship immediately settled by the stern with a list of 22° before ultimately capsizing, remaining afloat for 21 minutes before sinking. Eight officers and 80 ratings were lost. The survivors were picked up by the escorting destroyers *Aldenham*, *Beaufort*, and *Exmoor*, and were landed at Alexandria.

Euryalus was built at Chatham Dockyard, the last cruiser built there, being launched on 6 June 1939, and commissioned on 30 June 1941. She completed with her designed armament but in August 1941, at the end of work-up, she was taken in hand for a refit to replace damaged propellers. The opportunity was taken to replace the quadruple 0.5in machine gun mountings with five single 20mm Oerlikon guns.

In April 1943, *Euryalus* was under refit at Alexandria when changes were made to her radar equipment. The original radar Type 279 for air warning was replaced by Type 281 and Type 285 fitted for AA armament fire-control.

Between November 1943 and May 1944 she underwent a major refit and moderni-

Hermione in January 1942, with her primary armament as originally designed and upgraded close-in weapons.

Euryalus as completed in 1941 with full as-designed armament.

sation at John Brown Shipyard, Clydebank. 'Q' turret was removed and replaced by a quadruple pom-pom mounting to reduce top-weight. She was fitted with an Aircraft Direction Room for future use as an Escort Carrier Squadron Flagship. New design radars, Types 277 and 293 with interrogation equipment, replaced Type 272 for surface warning and height-finding. She also received new light anti-aircraft armament of six twin 20mm mountings, two replacing single mountings.

Euryalus remained in the British Pacific Fleet until returning to Great Britain in February 1947. She was reduced to reserve status at Rosyth and underwent a year-long modernisation in 1947–48. Her long-range air-warning radar set was changed to the late-war Type 279b/281. Her 5.25in turrets were also modified externally with the insertion of a large Perspex sighting window for the operators.

After service in the Mediterranean, Persian Gulf and South Atlantic, *Euryalus* paid off in 1954 and rejoined the reserve fleet at Devonport until sold to BISCO for demolition at Blyth in October 1958, arriving at the breaker's yard in tow on 18 July 1959.

Charybdis was the next of the class to commission, on 3 December 1941. She was

built by Cammell Laird, Birkenhead and launched on 17 September 1940.

Because of delays in the manufacture of guns, she was armed with four twin QF 4.5in Mk III turrets instead of the 5.25in guns. These 4.5in guns had originally been intended for upgrading the *Danae* class cruisers. There was no LA DCT for these guns and so *Charybdis* was fitted with two HA/LA DCTs, one forward and one aft.

She also had a single QF 4in Mk V gun for star-shell forward of 'X' mounting. The forward superstructure was considerably modified to accommodate these mountings, and also to increase crew spaces. *Charybdis* also carried the same surface armament as the others, six 21in torpedo tubes in two triple banks on the main deck, adjacent to the aft funnel. Her standard displacement was 5582 tons.

Her light AA at completion was four 20mm, and two single 2pdr pom-poms forward of the bridge. The 4in star-shell gun and the single 2pdr pom-poms were removed and replaced by two twin and two single 20mm, in 1942.

Originally fitted with radar Type 281, in 1942 a surface warning set Type 272 was added on the foremast. Radar ranging sets Type 285 and Type 282, two of each, were also fitted on completion.

Charybdis was assigned to Operation Tunnel to intercept the German blockade runner *Münsterland*, on 20 October 1943, together with six destroyers. The German vessel was accompanied by five Type 39 torpedo boats. *Charybdis* picked up the convoy on her radar at a range of 7nm, but at 0138 she was spotted by *T23* who, together with *T27*, fired a salvo of six torpedoes. *Charybdis* was hit on the port side by two torpedoes and sank within half an hour, with the loss of over 400 men. The first torpedo hit her port side, flooding No 2 dynamo room and 'B' boiler room and putting the after propulsion unit out of action. The second torpedo struck the ship

A good view of the two forward twin 4.5in gun turrets on *Charybdis*.

at about 135 station, displacing the after director and flooding the after engine room; all electric light failed and, in about five minutes, the list had increased to some 50°.

Cleopatra was built by R and W Hawthorn, Leslie and Company, Limited, Hebburn-on-Tyne, being launched on 27 March 1940, and commissioned on 5 December 1941.

She was completed as designed but with two single 2pdr pom-poms in place of the 0.5in machine guns and three single 20mm guns. She was fitted with radar Type 281. At this time her standard displacement was 5582 tons. In 1942, single 20mm guns replaced the single pom-poms, and in 1943 both 'Q' turret and the multiple pom-poms were removed and replaced by three American quadruple 40mm Bofors mountings. Four more single 20mm guns were also added. The following year, six twin 20mm mountings replaced five single mountings. During a refit from 1946 to 1951, the quadruple Bofors and Oerlikons were replaced by three twin Mk 5 Bofors and eight single Mk 7 Bofors mountings.

At the end of the war, *Cleopatra* remained in the East Indies until 7 January 1946. In June 1953 she attended the Coronation Review before going into reserve at Chatham, and between 1954 and 1956 she was used as Flagship for the Reserve Fleet at Portsmouth. She was placed on the Disposal List in 1958 and sold to BISCO for demolition by Cashmore at Newport, arriving at the breaker's yard on 15 December.

Sirius was built by Portsmouth Dockyard, but completion was delayed due to German bombing of the yard, so she was completed at Scotts Shipbuilding and Engineering Company, Greenock. She was launched on 18 September 1940, but not commissioned until 6 May 1942, when her displacement was 5785 tons.

Sirius was completed with five twin 5.25in turrets and five single 20mm Oerlikon guns. She had received two more 20mm by mid-1943. In 1944, three 20mm guns were landed and three 40mm Bofors Mk III guns were fitted. She was listed as having only seven 20mm as light AA in April 1944, and by April 1945 two more Mk III 40mm Bofors guns had been fitted.

Sirius survived the war, being deployed in the Mediterranean until February 1946 when she took passage to Great Britain for a refit. She was laid up during the manning shortage in 1947 but re-commissioned the next year. Paid off in April 1949, she was reduced to reserve. After six years in the Reserve Fleet, *Sirius* was placed on the Disposal List and sold to BISCO for breaking up by Hughes Bolckow at Blyth where she arrived on 15 October 1956.

Scylla, like *Charybdis*, was completed with four twin 4.5in Mk III in UD Mk III mountings because of a shortage of 5.25in mountings. Her light AA on completion was eight

Sirius as completed.

single 20mm guns. These were sited in pairs on either side of the ship, forward of the bridge, in the bridge wings, adjacent to the aft DCT, and forward of 'X' turret. One other noticeable difference in these two vessels when compared to their sisters, was the installation of a boat crane amidships, between the two funnels.

Scylla was built by Scotts Shipbuilding and Engineering Company, Greenock, being launched on 24 July 1940 and commissioned on 12 June 1942. Her original radar outfit was the same as that of *Charybdis*, but she did not receive the Type 272. Six twin power-operated 20mm guns were added in 1944.

Whilst involved in operations off Sword Beach, on 23 June 1944 *Scylla* was badly damaged by a mine in six fathoms of water off the beachhead. She sustained major damage to her starboard keel structure adjacent to the machinery compartments, the turbine casings were cracked, and she was without electric power.

Towed to Chatham, a survey found the damage to be uneconomic to repair and *Scylla* was held in the reserve fleet until 1948 when she was placed on the Disposal List. Later that year she was used for ship target trials before being sold to BISCO for demolition at Barrow by Vickers. She arrived at the breakers' yard on 6 May 1950.

Argonaut, the last of the original class to commission, was constructed at the Cammell Laird shipyard, Birkenhead, being launched on 6 September 1941, and commissioned into service on 8 August 1942.

She completed as designed but with four single 20mm in place of the 0.5in machine guns, displacing 5972 tons standard. Her after funnel was cut-down by two feet to reduce weight. In 1943, the single 20mm guns were replaced by twins, and in 1944, she had 'Q' turret removed and replaced by a quadruple 2pdr pom-pom, and five single 20mm guns were added. In 1945 an additional 20mm gun was installed, the twin 20mm guns were adapted to carry a 40mm gun ('Boffin') mounting, four 40mm guns were added and two 20mm removed.

Argonaut received a full radar outfit of Type 272, Type 281, ranging set Type 284, two ranging sets Type 285, and two ranging sets Type 282. During 1942–43, the vessels completed earlier were all brought up to the same standard. Eventually, Type 272 was replaced by Type 277, and IFF sets 242 and 252 were added for use with Type 272, and IFF sets 240 and 243 for use with Type 281.

On 14 December 1942, *Argonaut* was heavily damaged when struck by two torpedoes, from a spread of four, fired by the Italian submarine *Lazzaro Mocenigo*. The bow and stern sections of the cruiser were effectively blown off and the steering wrecked. The German authorities mistakenly believed she had been sunk. Three crew members were killed. The ship was patched up and limped to Algiers for more temporary repairs, before sailing to the United States, where she underwent a seven-month reconstruction, completed in November 1943.

On return to Great Britain, *Argonaut* received the new Type 293 and 277 radars. She took part in bombardment duties on D-Day and also supported the Allied invasion of Southern France, Operation Dragoon, before joining the British Pacific Fleet in 1945. She returned to Portsmouth in 1946 and was reduced to reserve status and laid-up, being placed on the Disposal List in 1955. She was sold to BISCO for demolition by J Cashmore and arrived at the breaker's yard in Newport in November 1955.

BELLONA CLASS CRUISERS

The five ships in the *Bellona* class had all been ordered and laid down as members of the *Dido* class, 1939 programme. Because of both material and labour shortages, they were suspended in 1940–41, and when construction re-started, they were all completed to a modified design.

They received the same radar fit as *Argonaut*, and remote power control was fitted to both the 5.25in turrets and the multiple 2pdr pom-pom mountings. 'Q' turret was omitted and replaced by a third pom-pom mounting with its director and a third Type 282 radar set. This reduced topweight and allowed the superstructure to be lowered and rearranged, further reducing topweight. The revised superstructure allowed both the funnels and masts to be vertical, rather than raked, the funnels also being shorter. A deckhouse was added between the funnels. The ships were all fitted with Asdic.

All of the class used the High Angle Control System (HACS) to remotely control their 5.25in guns. Close-range protection was enhanced by the inclusion of six twin 20mm Oerlikon mountings. All the ships were completed as designed and, although some received changes to their armament, none received any changes to the radar outfit.

The design standard displacement was 5770 tons, but *Spartan*, the lead ship, completed at 6018 tons.

Spartan was built by Vickers-Armstrongs at Barrow-in-Furness, being launched on 27 August 1942 and commissioned at Devonport on 10 August 1943.

She received no modification before her loss on 29 January 1944: at about 1800, a radio-controlled Henschel Hs 293 glide bomb hit her just aft of the after funnel and detonated high up in the compartments abreast the port side of the after boiler room, blowing a large hole in the upper deck. The main mast collapsed and the boiler rooms were flooded. Steam and electrical power failed, a serious fire developed and the ship heeled over to port. About an hour after being hit, *Spartan* had to be abandoned, and 10 minutes later she settled on her beam ends in about 25–30ft of water. Five officers and 41 ratings were posted killed or missing presumed killed, and 42 ratings were wounded.

Royalist was built by Scotts Shipbuilding and Engineering Company of Greenock, being launched on 30 May 1942, and commissioned on 10 September 1943. She returned to the dockyard for modification, with extra facilities and crew for operating as a flagship in aircraft carrier operations, in November, and this was not completed until February 1944.

She received two twin and four single 20mm guns and in 1945 four more singles

Royalist paying-off in January 1946.

were added. Her torpedo tubes were removed in 1944 to save weight.

She was withdrawn from the East Indies after the end of the war and returned home to be mothballed in 1946. The Admiralty ordered the modernisation of four *Dido* class cruisers in 1950, and *Royalist* was planned to be the first, with work scheduled to start in January 1953. The modernisation required the construction of a new superstructure and the addition of a fire control system, and, in March 1953, the reconstruction of *Royalist* began. With a change in government following the general election of 1951, the Admiralty's budget was cut in 1952. Under these financial cuts, plans to refurbish *Royalist* and her sister ships were postponed and later cancelled.

She was handed over to the Royal New Zealand Navy, on loan, on 9 July 1956 following the completion of a refurbishment, at a cost of £4.5 million. As part of the New Zealand half of her refurbishment, *Royalist* was fitted with a new radar, fire control system, and three 'STAAG 2' 40mm anti-aircraft mountings. She was paid off on 4 June 1966 and, after eleven years in the RNZN, reverted to Royal Navy control. She was sold for scrap to the Nissho Company of Japan in November 1967. She was then towed from Auckland to Osaka on 31 December 1967 and scrapped upon arrival.

Bellona was built by Fairfield Shipbuilding and Engineering Company, Govan, being launched on 29 September 1942 and commissioned on 29 October 1943. By 1945, *Bellona* was fitted with six single 20mm guns.

She survived the war and in 1946, she was loaned to the Royal New Zealand Navy. By 1952 a limited attempt at modernisation was undertaken, when the Oerlikons were replaced with land Mk III single 40mm Bofors guns, upgraded with electric power to the RNZN's own 'Toadstool' CIWS.

Bellona reverted to Royal Navy control after the transfer of the cruiser *Royalist* in 1956. The multiple pom-pom mounts were reinstalled for the return voyage to the UK as the RN judged 'Toadstool' as non-standard and not as good as the RN's new electric 40mm mounts. She was in reserve between 1956 and 1957 and was sent to Briton Ferry for breaking up in February 1959.

Black Prince was built by Harland & Wolff of Belfast, being launched on 27 August 1942, and completed on 20 November 1943. Her standard displacement was 6000 tons.

By 1945, her AA armament had been increased to eight single 20mm guns, and later, four of these were replaced by two single 40mm guns. After the Japanese surrender, *Black Prince* remained in the Far East, and was transferred to the Royal New Zealand Navy on 25 May 1946. During 1947, she was docked for modernisation, but this was cancelled as the RNZN no longer had the manpower to operate her, and she was placed in reserve. Work on reactivating the ship began in January 1952, when the two multiple pom-pom mounts were removed and she had eight 40mm Bofors Mk IIIP 'Toadstool' Systems fitted before recommissioning in February 1953.

Black Prince was decommissioned again in August 1955 and used as an accommodation ship for refitting warships and a spare parts source for the 1960–61 refit of *Royalist*. She was sold for scrap in March 1962 and towed to the Mitsui & Company, Osaka breaking yards, arriving there on 2 May 1962.

Diadem was built by Hawthorn Leslie and Company at Hebburn-on-Tyne, Yard Number 624, being launched on 26 August 1942, and completed on 6 January 1944. By the end of the war, she carried ten 20mm guns, two twins and six singles.

She was placed in reserve between 1950 and 1956, and sold to the Pakistan Navy on 29 February 1956, being refitted at Portsmouth Dockyard before being handed over and renamed *Babur* on 5 July 1957. The refit included fourteen 40mm/L60 guns in three twin Mk 5 mounts and eight single Mk 7 mounts. Radar was updated to Type 974 navigation, Type 293 target indicator and metric air warning set with combined Tx/Rx antenna, air warning, Type 281B. She retained Type 984/985. The air conditioning was modified for use in the tropics and a new bridge was fitted. The cost of the refit far exceeded Pakistan's ability to pay and defence cuts saw her temporarily laid up as a fully manned static training ship for cadets in 1961. However, *Babur* was back in full operational service by 1963. Renamed *Jahangir* in 1982, she was broken up in 1985.

■ *DIDO* AND *BELLONA* CLASSES: PRINCIPAL PARTICULARS

	DIDO CLASS	**BELLONA** CLASS
Number in class	11	5
Displacement (tons)		
Standard	5450	5770
Deep Load	6836	7350
Length Overall	512ft	512ft
Beam	50ft 6in	50ft 6in
Machinery	4-shaft Parsons geared turbines, 62,000shp	4-shaft Parsons geared turbines, 62,000shp
Speed (at standard displacement)	32.25 knots	32 knots
Primary Armament	Ten 5.25in QF Mk I in five twin turrets Mk II	Eight 5.25in QF Mk I in four twin turrets Mk II
Star-shell	–	One 4in Mk I
Secondary armament	Eight 2pdr (40mm) Mk VIII 'pom-pom' in two quadruple Mk VII mountings	Eight 2pdr (40mm) Mk VIII 'pom-pom' in two quadruple Mk VII mountings
Close-in armament	Eight 0.5in Mk III machine guns in two quadruple Mk III mountings	Eight 0.5in Mk III machine guns in two quadruple Mk III mountings
Torpedo tubes	Two triple 21in mountings	Two triple 21in mountings

CAMOUFLAGE

Coventry. When first converted, she was painted in MS4a overall, with 'holystoned' wood decks. In 1940, she received a darker grey scheme of 507a/G10, with a white false bow wave. The decks were still wood, although no longer 'holystoned'. The next year, *Coventry* had some areas overpainted in a lighter grey B55, the patterns on the two sides being similar, but not identical. Metal decks were painted dark grey. After her refit in Bombay in 1942, the pattern changed, although the same two colours were retained. It is probable that the decks were painted grey at this time.

Curlew. After her conversion, *Curlew* appeared similar to *Coventry* (MS4a) and was also painted in 507a/G10 at the beginning of war. At the time of her loss, limited areas of her superstructure and funnels had been overpainted in 507c.

Cairo. Painted in 507a at the beginning of the war, *Cairo* soon received an extensive white bow wave. In mid-1940 she received some areas of 507c, in a 'dazzle' type pattern of her own design. She is reported to have been painted dark grey overall during the Norwegian campaign. The following year, she received an Admiralty Disruptive pattern using 507c, MS3 and 507a. Decks were still wood, although not 'holystoned'. The design was modified during her last refit, although colours remained the same.

Calcutta. Initially *Calcutta* received a less extensive bow wave. Shortly before her loss she was painted in an unofficial complicated scheme of 507a, 507b and 507c.

Carlisle. Like her sisters, *Carlisle* was painted in 507a overall at the beginning of the war but was repainted in 507c when sent to the Red Sea in 1940. In 1941, while in the Mediterranean, she received a complicated, unofficial pattern in 507a and 507c. This pattern was simplified in early 1942, and the following year, she received an Admiralty Disruptive scheme in G10 and B55, gunshield roofs were G10.

Curacoa. In mid-1940, *Curacoa* was painted in 507b overall, and she was repainted in 507a after the Norwegian campaign. Shortly before her loss, she was painted in medium 'Mountbatten pink', with light grey countershading under the flare of the bow. She is the only cruiser known to have carried a pennant number, D41.

Colombo. In home waters, *Colombo* was painted MS4a overall, changing to 507c when sent to the Far East. In November 1941, before her conversion, she had a dark grey, 507a, hull, this colour also being used on small parts of her superstructure. The rest of her was painted in 507c. When converted, she was given a camouflage pattern that used white, B5 and MS2, with dark grey (507a?) decks. Towards the end of the war, *Colombo* was painted in B55, with a coloured panel of B30 on the hull. Decks were wood, with horizontal metal surfaces painted B55. Mast tops were white.

Coventry sporting an elaborate false bow wave.

Caledon. In 1941, *Caledon* received a simple camouflage scheme of 507c and 507a. When converted, she received a scheme which used green G45 as a base, with areas of G10 and B15, retaining this scheme until decommissioned.

Delhi. When converted, *Delhi* received a disruptive camouflage scheme using 507c as a base, with areas of B5 and 507a. Decks were mid-grey. By mid-1943, she was painted in 507b overall but then received a three-colour Admiralty disruptive scheme which was soon simplified to use G45 and G10. Gunshield roofs were G10. When refitted at Gibraltar in 1944, her hull was painted MS2 with MS3 upperworks.

Bonaventure. When first commissioned, *Bonaventure* was painted in 507b, with turret tops in 507c. Decks were wood with other horizontal surfaces painted 507b. In early 1941, she received a simple camouflage scheme of 507c as a base, with areas of 507a, the pattern being identical port and starboard. The top of 'Y' turret was painted in 507a. By the time of her loss, the areas of 507a had been extended.

Naiad. Upon completion, *Naiad* received a short-lived scheme of brown, green and white, that was thought to be suitable for ships based at Scapa Flow. She soon received a scheme using black, 507b and 507c. the areas being similar to those of the previous pattern. By the time of her loss, *Naiad* had a hull of 507b, with upperworks in 507c. The decks and horizontal surfaces were all 507b.

Dido. Originally painted in 507b overall, including horizontal metal surfaces, she was repainted in MS4a when undergoing repairs in the USA. Decks were wood and the horizontal metal surfaces remained in 507b. She did receive at least two different camouflage schemes for short periods of time, but by mid-1943, her hull was painted in 507b with 507c superstructure. 'A' turret, 'Y' turret and the fore-funnel were painted 507b, with 507c turret tops and wood decks. Later in the war, while protecting convoys to and from Russia, she wore a MS2 hull, with G45 upperworks and horizontal surfaces, the decks remaining unpainted.

Phoebe. Like *Naiad*, when first commissioned *Phoebe* received a brown and green pattern, but in this case, the only white was a small bow wave. From late 1940 until early 1942, *Phoebe* wore a simple camouflage scheme with 507c as the base, overpainted with areas of 507b. All horizontal surfaces, including turret tops, were painted 507b and the top sections of the masts were painted white. After repairs in the USA, she reappeared in a similar scheme to that worn by *Dido* – 507b hull, fore-funnel, 'A' and 'Y' turret, with 507c upperworks. All decks were 507b.

After her second set of repairs in the USA in 1943, *Phoebe* (minus 'A' turret) appeared with 507a hull and horizontal surfaces and 507c upperworks. On her return to Great Britain, she reverted to her previous pattern, but with 507a being used instead of 507b. Upon going east in 1944, she was painted 507c overall, with a blue hull panel. The horizontal surfaces remained in 507a, and the turret tops were painted to match.

Hermione. The ship completed in medium grey overall, but a complicated scheme using B55, B5, MS3, MS4a, 507c and 507a was applied in early 1942. Within two months, this changed to 507a hull and decks with 507b upperworks. In the Mediterranean in late 1941, she was painted medium 'Mountbatten pink'.

Euryalus. She commissioned wearing a similar complicated camouflage scheme to *Hemione*, the same colours being used. Similarly, she also changed to 507b hull and decks with 507c upperworks, including all turrets, within three months. In the Mediterranean she had a simple camouflage scheme of 507c, overpainted with areas of 507a. From mid-1942, *Euryalus* adopted the standard 507b hull, fore-funnel, 'A' and 'Y' turrets, with 507c upperworks. Following her major refit in 1943–44, she appeared with a B30 hull and G45 upperworks, decks being 507a.

On joining the BPF in 1945, *Euryalus* was painted 507c overall with a B15 hull panel and 507a decks.

Charybdis. *Charybdis* commissioned with a complicated scheme of green, MS1, MS3 and white, decks being 507b. In 1942, she was repainted in a simpler scheme of MS2, MS3 and white, with 507a decks.

Cleopatra. Completed in a complicated scheme involving MS1, B5, B6 and MS4a, she changed to a simpler pattern of MS3, 507a and 507c in mid-1942. In both cases, decks were wood with horizontal metal surfaces MS4a. After her repairs in late 1944, she was painted in 507c, with a blue hull panel, and 507a decks.

Sirius. *Sirius* entered service with a complicated Admiralty Disruptive scheme using B5, MS4, MS4a and MS2, with 507a decks. In late 1942, this was simplified by removing B5. Turret tops were MS4a in both cases. In early 1944, she had a dark grey hull 507a, up to the level of the main deck. The upper forebody was MS4a, as were the upperworks. In 1945, she adopted a darker scheme of B20 and MS2.

Scylla. *Scylla* carried just one camouflage scheme, an Admiralty disruptive scheme using MS2, MS3 and white. Wooden decks were painted pale grey, with metal areas 507b. The tops of 'A' and 'B' gun shields

Scylla in June 1942

were 507c, while those of 'X' and 'Y' were MS3.

Argonaut commissioned wearing an Admiralty Disruptive scheme using B6, 507a and 507c, decks and turret tops being in 507a. Later in the year, the scheme changed to include B5, B6, MS1 and 507c. When repaired in the USA, she was repainted 507b (or an equivalent American colour) overall, and in Home Fleet service she had a 507b hull and turret tops, with the superstructure in 507c. When sent to the Pacific in late 1944, she was 507c overall with a hull panel in B5. In 1945, the panel was changed to B15.

Spartan wore just one camouflage pattern using B30, B55 and G10. Decks and horizontal surfaces were B10.

Royalist wore a three-colour pattern – B55,

B30 and G10 – with G10 decks. Turret tops were B55 ('A'), and G10 ('B', 'X' and 'Y'). Whilst with the Eastern Fleet, this was changed to 507c overall, with a B20 hull panel.

Bellona completed in a pattern using the same three colours as *Royalist*. Turret tops were B30 ('A'), B55 ('B') and G10 ('X' and 'Y'). On D-Day she had her hull and horizontal surfaces, including the turret tops, painted G10, with superstructure painted MS3.

Black Prince. Upon completion, *Black Prince* appeared similar to both *Royalist* and *Bellona*. By late 1944, her hull was painted B30, with her upperworks MS4a.

Diadem first appeared in a pattern similar to those of her sisters, later in the war changing to G45 overall with a B20 hull panel. Decks were G10.

Argonaut in 1942.

Bellona in November 1943.

HMS *Cairo* as completed

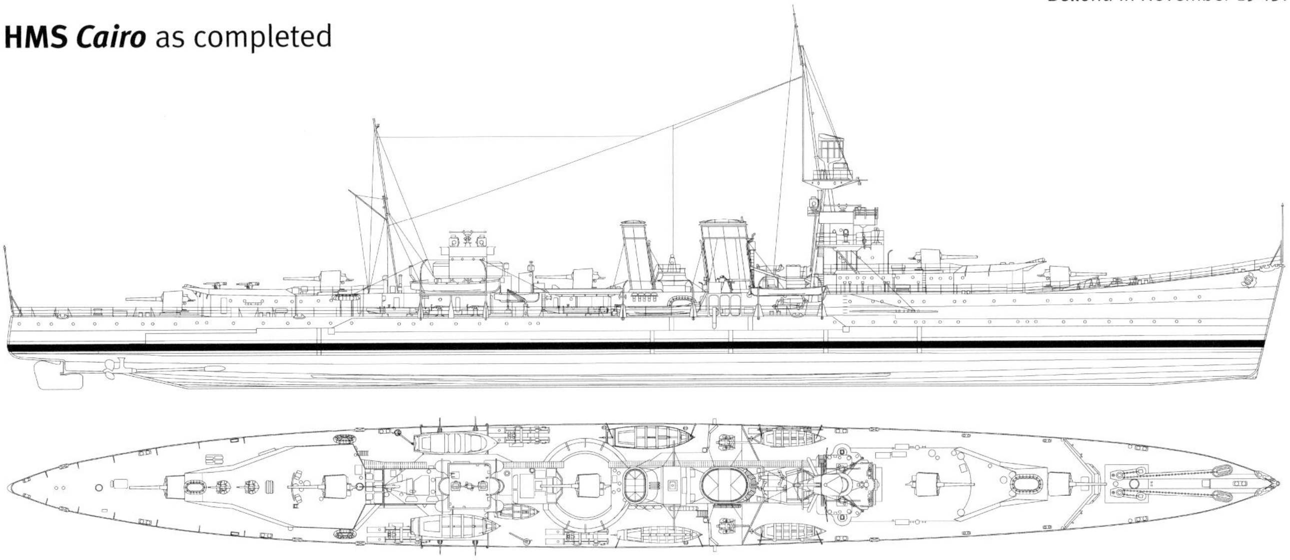

HMS *Curacoa* 1918

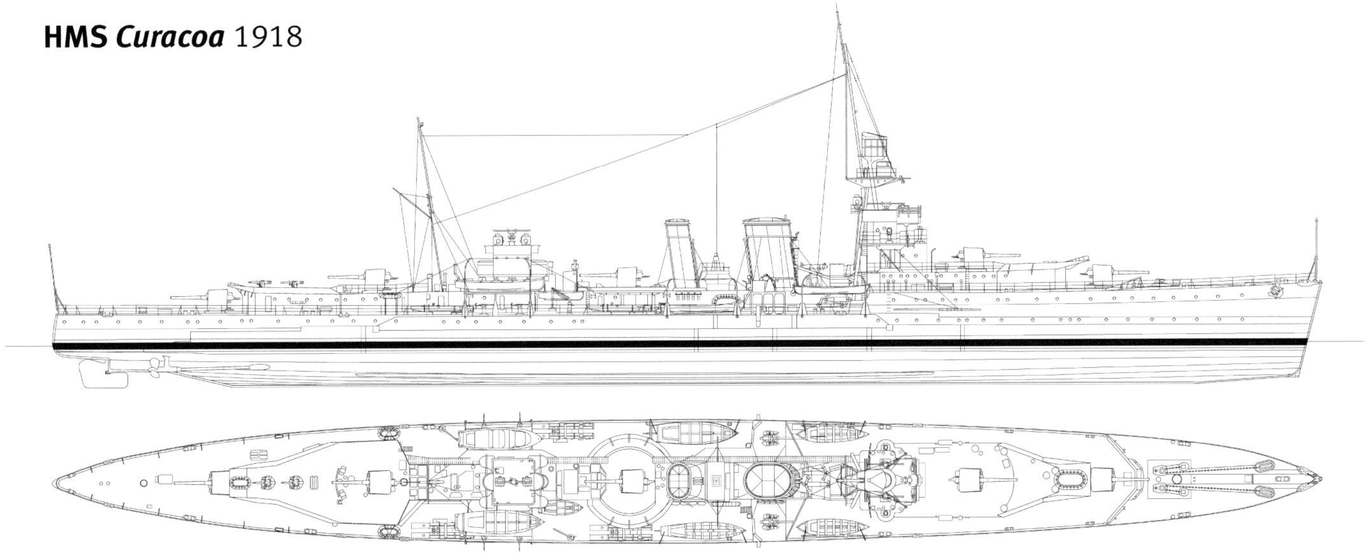

HMS *Coventry* 1936

HMS *Coventry* 1940

HMS *Calcutta* 1939

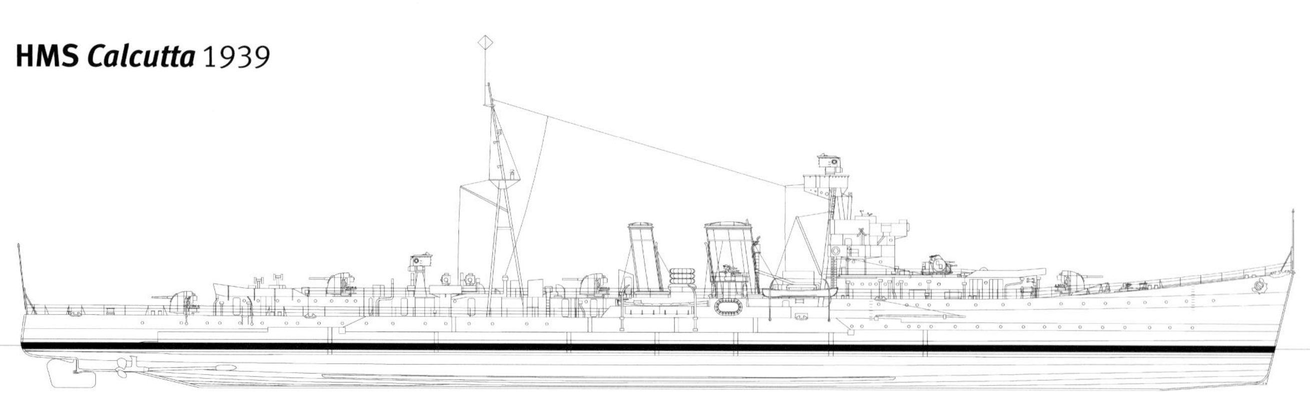

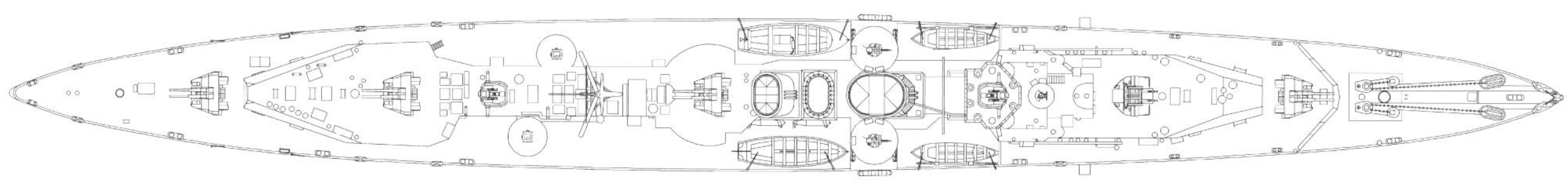

HMS *Colombo* 1943

HMS *Delhi* as completed

HMS *Delhi* 1943

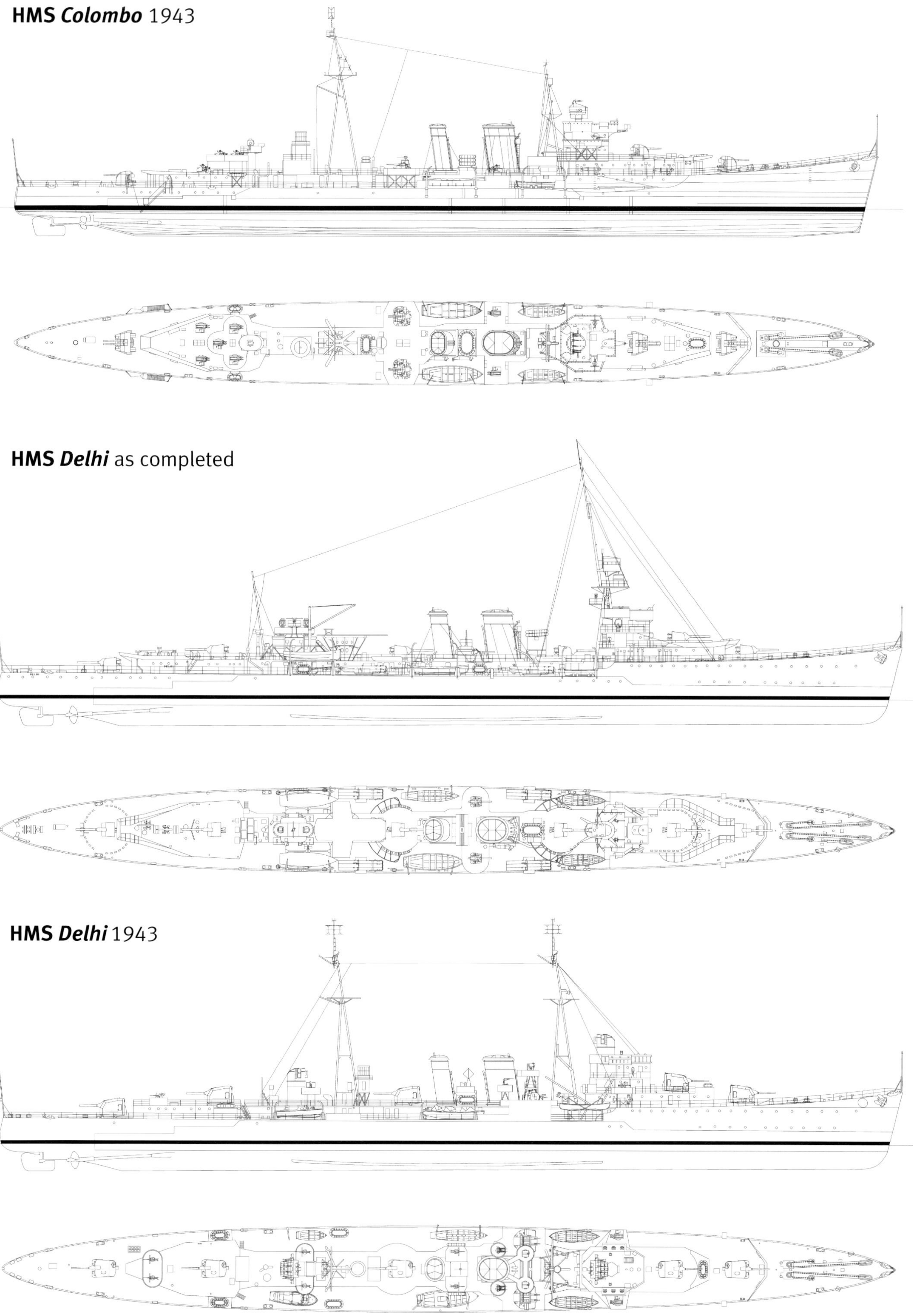

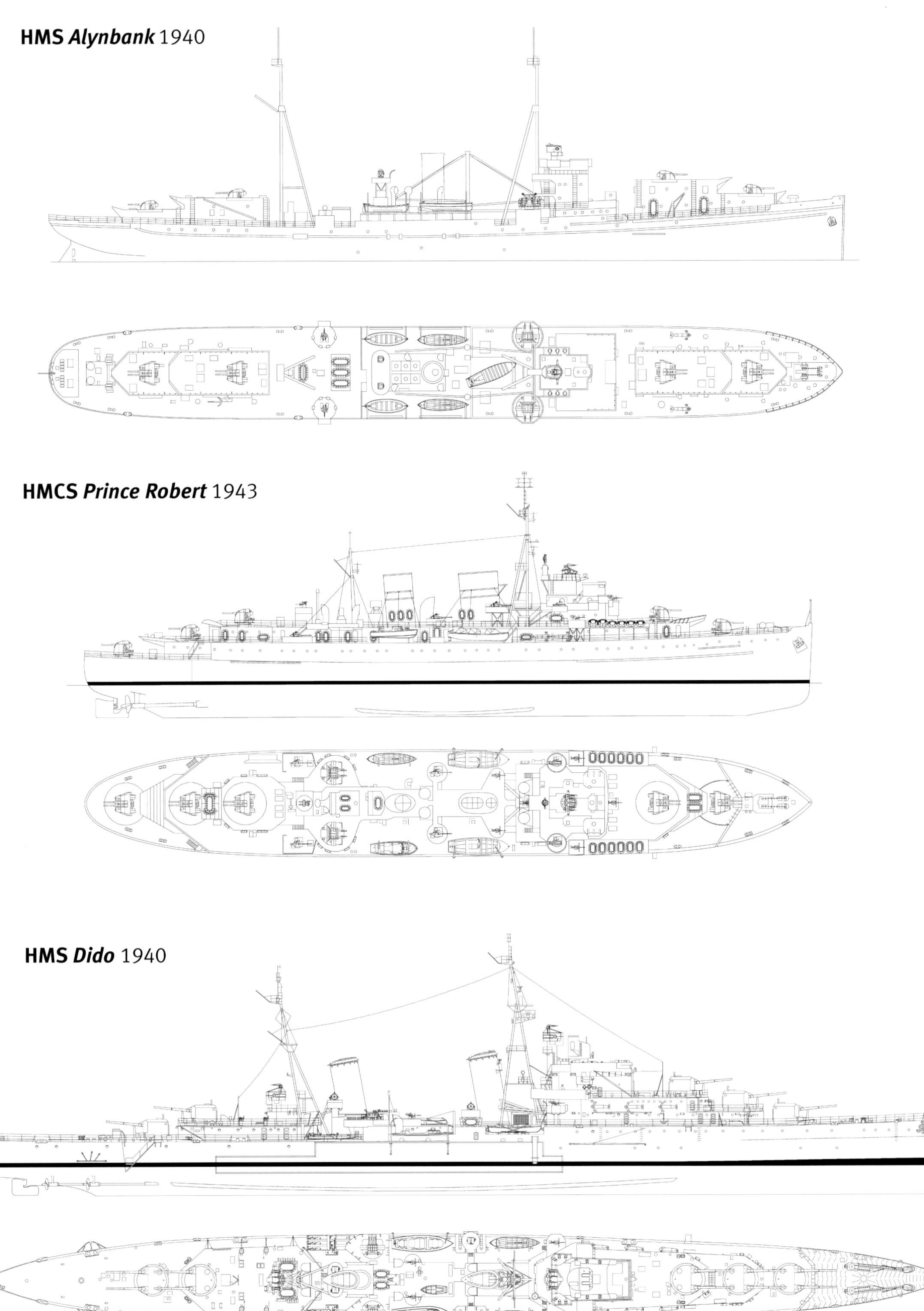

HMS *Alynbank* 1940
HMCS *Prince Robert* 1943
HMS *Dido* 1940

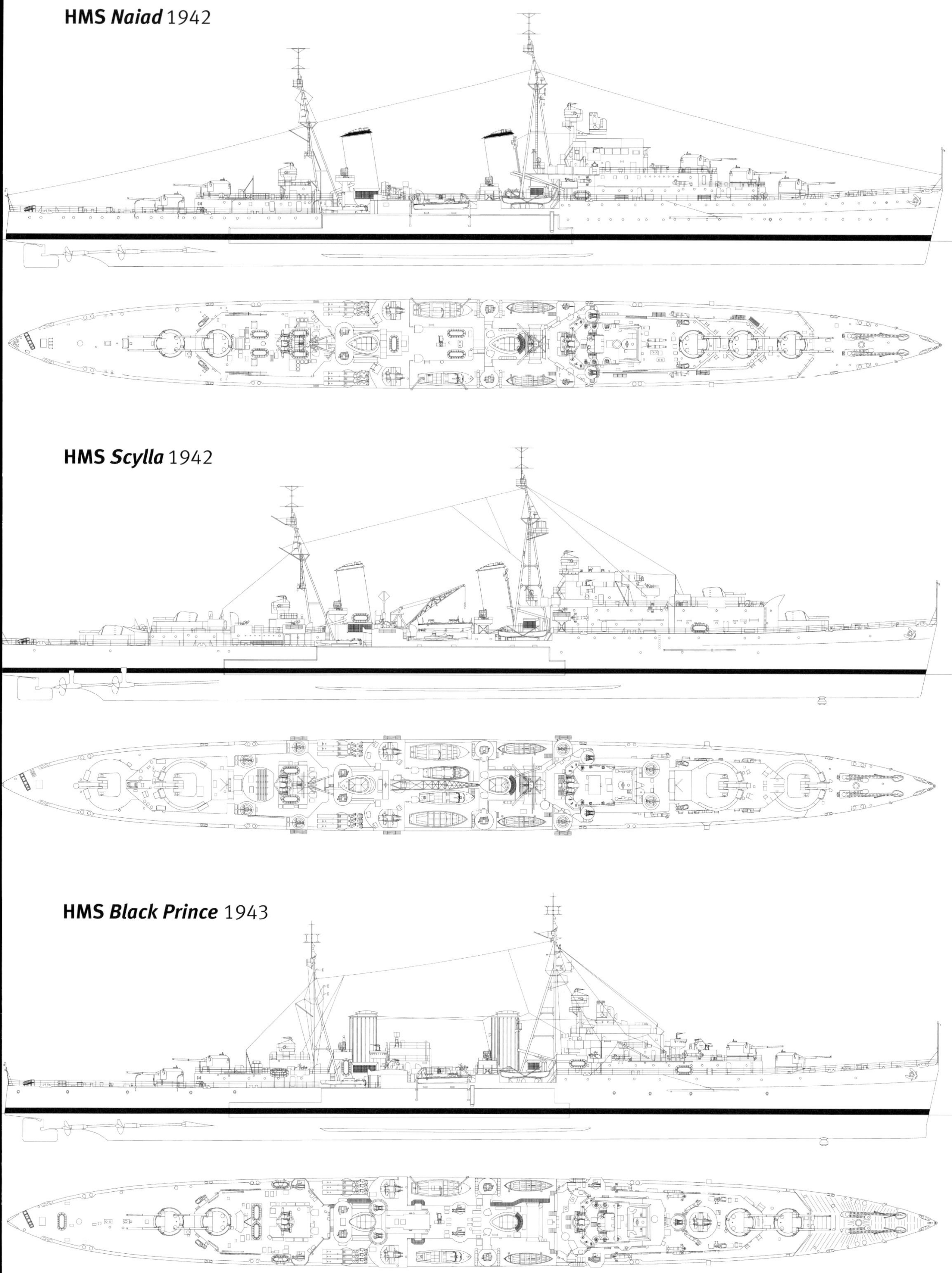

HMS *Naiad* 1942
HMS *Scylla* 1942
HMS *Black Prince* 1943

Selected References

BIBLIOGRAPHY

100 Years of Specialized Shipbuilding & Engineering, by K C Barnaby (Hutchinson, 1964)

Armed Merchant Cruisers, by Richard Osborne, Harry Spong & Tom Grover (World Ship Society, 2007)

British and Commonwealth Warship Camouflage of WWII, Volume 3, by Malcolm Wright (Seaforth Publishing, 2016)

British Cruisers: Two World Wars and After, by Norman Friedman (Seaforth Publishing, 2010)

British Cruisers of World War Two, by Alan Raven & John Roberts (Arms and Armour Press, 1980)

Conway's All the World's Fighting Ships, 1906-1921, edited by Randal Gray (Conway Maritime Press, 1985)

Conway's All the World's Fighting Ships, 1922-1946, edited by Roger Chesneau (Conway Maritime Press, 1980)

Cruisers In Action, 1939-1945, by Peter Smith & John R Dominey (William Kimber & Co, 1981)

Ensign 2: Dido Class Cruisers, by Alan Raven & H T Lenton (Bivouac Books Ltd, 1973)

HMS Dido – a Tiffy's Tale, by Eric Jeffs (Arthur H Stockwell Ltd, 2005)

Profile Morskie 12: British Cruiser Scylla, by S Brzeziński (Firma Wydawniczo-Handlowa, 1998)

Profile Morskie 38: British Cruiser Calcutta, by J Mościński & S Brzeziński (Firma Wydawniczo-Handlowa, 2001)

Profile Morskie 40: British Antiaircraft Cruiser Delhi, by J Mościński & S Brzeziński (Firma Wydawniczo-Handlowa, 2001)

Profile Morskie 48: British AA Cruiser Colombo, by J Mościński & S Brzeziński (Firma Wydawniczo-Handlowa, 2002)

Profile Morskie 67: British AA Cruiser Naiad, by S Brzeziński (Firma Wydawniczo-Handlowa, 2004)

Profile Morskie 69: British AA Cruiser Argonaut, by S Brzeziński (Firma Wydawniczo-Handlowa, 2005)

Profile Morskie 89: British AA Cruiser Coventry, by J Mościński & S Brzeziński (Firma Wydawniczo-Handlowa, 2004)

Ships of the Royal Navy, by J J College, Ben Warlow & Steve Bush (Seaforth Publishing, 2020)

Valiant Quartet: His Majesty's Anti-Aircraft Cruisers Curlew, Cairo, Calcutta and Coventry, by G G Connell (William Kimber & Co, 1979)

Warship Perspectives, Camouflage Volume One: Royal Navy 1939-1941, by Alan Raven (WR Press Inc, 2000)

Warship Perspectives, Camouflage Volume Two: Royal Navy 1942, by Alan Raven (WR Press Inc, 2001)

Warship Perspectives, Camouflage Volume Three: Royal Navy 1943-1944, by Alan Raven (WR Press Inc, 2001)

MANUFACTURERS' WEBSITES

https://www.navis-neptun.de
https://www.combrig-models.com
https://micromaster.co.nz
http://ajmmodels.pl
https://www.atlanticmodels.net
https://trumpetermodels.com
https://nikomodel.pl
https://blackcatmodels.eu
https://starlingmodels.co.uk
http://wsw-modellbau.de
http://www.flyhawkmodel.com
https://www.swordfishmodels.com
https://nntmodell.com

Diadem at the end of the war carrying a darker hull panel.